"William Attaway
new book, enti
many books on the topic of leadership these days, most of
them striving to focus on one of the many, various aspects of
this discipline. However, William takes on the very difficult
task of providing a broader approach by describing the twelve
keys to becoming an intentional leader that makes a difference.
He hits this topic 'out of the park,' first of all, by carefully
choosing twelve essential principles. Then, William examines
each of these principles in a very practical, down-to-earth,
easy-to- read fashion, weaving together the wisdom of a
variety of the best leaders in the world. Every leader would
benefit greatly from the strategic insights of this book."

--Dee Whitten, Executive Director, Northstar Church Network

"Catalytic Leadership is the result of decades of disciplined
learning and execution. It is accessible and offers avenues of
application for leaders of all varieties and scope. This volume
necessarily bridges the spheres of conceptual leadership and
the relentless daily grind of actually leading others and self. Dr.
Attaway's burden for humble leadership and organizations that
are characterized by the same humility and clarity resonates
throughout every chapter. The tenets found in these pages are
tried, proven, and worthy of revisiting regularly."

--Dr. Mike Watson, Senior Associate Pastor of Ministries,
Second Baptist Church, Springfield, MO

"You will not find a more dedicated, passionate, and thorough student of leadership than William Attaway. Catalytic Leadership provides an invaluable resource for all leaders, regardless of experience or industry, whereby they can take a deep look within and unleash personal and organizational transformation. Acknowledging his own leadership journey and struggles, William invites the reader to come alongside as he deftly synthesizes some of the best and most innovative leadership principles in practice today. At a time when leaders in all arenas face intense scrutiny and skepticism, this book outlines a refreshingly humble yet bold prescription for leadership success. My personal to-do list got dramatically revamped by this work, and thankfully so."

--Kevin Skillin, U.S. Diplomat

"Are you looking to grow yourself, your team, or your organization? If so, then this is the book for you. Dr. Attaway lays out a clear, concise, path to becoming a 'catalytic leader' in this book. I love the combination of the 12 Keys that he teaches that are both common-sense and practically based. Self-awareness, intentionality, self-leadership, and accountability are great for personal and professional development, but Dr. Attaway really encourages that for true growth being a 'river not a reservoir' – developing other leaders and passing along what you've learned. Couldn't recommend this book highly enough if you are truly looking to grow and develop as a leader who wants to make positive change!"

--David A. Miles, Ph.D., Founder | Principal, Dr. Dave Leadership Corporation

"William Attaway's Catalytic Leadership is a must for anyone who is intentional about developing and growing as a leader. This book is not abstract ideology. It is a comprehensive roadmap to help us understand what it takes to inspire those we are privileged to lead. To become agents who can provoke significant and powerful impact. To become catalytic leaders. This book crystalises what William has learned as a leader, working with real leaders in the real world. As one who has worked under William for a number of years, I have had the privilege of experiencing catalytic leadership in action. If your goal is to be a great leader, this is the book is for you.

--Rob Petrini, Executive Coach, Wilberforce Foundation / Senior Pastor, Hutt City Baptist Church

Catalytic Leadership

12 Keys To Becoming an Intentional Leader
Who Makes A Difference

William C. Attaway

Eriall Press

ERIALL PRESS

Catalytic Leadership: 12 Keys to Becoming an Intentional Leader Who Makes a Difference

William C. Attaway

Published in the United States by Eriall Press.

ISBN: 979-8-9855968-1-6 (paperback)
ISBN: 979-8-9855968-0-9 (e-book)

Visit CatalyticLeadership.net for more information.

This book is dedicated to my daughters, Erin and Allison, who I pray will be catalytic leaders in their generation.

I remind myself every morning: Nothing I say this day will teach me anything. So if I'm going to learn, I must do it by listening. I never learned anything while I was talking.

—Larry King

Contents

Introduction

*"The leaders who make the most progress
make the fewest excuses.
And the leaders who make the most excuses
make the least progress."*
— Carey Nieuwhof

When I was twelve, I got hit in the head with a baseball.

I was at bat, and the coach signaled for me to bunt. I'd done this many times in the past, and so I got ready. Something happened between my brain and my body, because my body didn't line up quite right and I missed the ball completely with my bat but managed to line up perfectly for it to hit me square in the forehead.

Ouch.

A trip to the hospital and a concussion diagnosis later, I was on my way home, bruised but glad to be okay.

As I listen to leaders these days, it's not uncommon for them to express that leadership feels to them a little like getting hit in the head with a baseball. You think you're lined up, doing the right thing, and then BAM! Out of the blue comes the ball, and you're on the ground.

I hear leaders describe their passion, their vision, their dream, and how they believe in what could be, what should be. But they're trapped by their own limiting beliefs holding them back, keeping them from the significance and impact they know is possible.

I talk with leaders who are working hard to make a difference. They want to lead for the benefit of others, not for themselves. But they're struggling to figure out how exactly to do that well in the midst of the day-to-day grind.

Have you ever felt that way?

Leadership is challenging. I know that firsthand. And I'm passionate about helping leaders intentionally grow and thrive in their leadership contexts.

When I became intentional about helping other leaders grow, I started a company called Catalytic Leadership. Why that name?

I was a pre-pharmacy major when I went to college. I had worked in a pharmacy at the end of high school, and because of that experience, I decided that would be my career aspiration. I loved the idea of devoting my life to helping people in practical ways.

I loved the idea—until I took chemistry. Those chicken-wire diagrams would haunt me in my sleep. Basic chemistry wasn't bad, but then we moved to inorganic and organic. And I realized that this was not what I wanted to do for the rest of my life.

I've learned that God never wastes an experience though. I discovered in my (brief) chemistry studies the power of a catalyst. A catalyst is something that sparks or accelerates significant change. Its impact is powerful and often difficult to reverse, if at all possible.

A catalytic leader, then, is one who sparks or accelerates significant change or action with a powerful impact.

I love that.

Every great leader I've ever met or learned from is a catalytic leader. They want to see significant change or action in their organizations, either in advancing their mission or in developing their team and other leaders. And they take action to make it so. They don't just react to the circumstances around them; they are proactive in changing the circumstances if they can. This type of leadership begins with the mindset of the leader.

I aspire to be a catalytic leader. For the last three decades, I've been a student of effective and impactful leadership. I'm a leadership coach who comes alongside leaders who want to be catalytic, and I help them to accomplish just that.

When I was fifteen years old, I attended my first leadership conference in Valley Forge, Pennsylvania. I was hooked.

For over thirty years now, I've read everything I could get my hands on that had anything to do with leadership: biographies of great leaders, books on business leadership, nonprofit leadership, church leadership, sports leadership, government leadership, and more articles than I can remember from *Harvard Business Review, Forbes,* the *Wall Street Journal, Leadership Journal,* and many others. I've attended scores of leadership conferences, hearing from thought leaders and practitioners of leadership in every facet of life. I've bought coffee and lunches for leaders who would agree to meet with me and let me ply them with question after question about how they lead and why they made the decisions they did in their own leadership journeys. And I've had the incredible privilege of being a member of the John Maxwell Team, learning from a man widely regarded as one of the great leadership thinkers in our world, John C. Maxwell. His prolific writing—over one hundred books to date—has influenced my life and leadership in inestimable ways, nor could I ever adequately convey my immense gratitude.

Brian Herbert said, "The capacity to learn is a gift; the ability to learn is a skill; the willingness to learn is a choice."[1] I have chosen to learn, now and forever. And I have chosen to invest in leaders who make that same choice.

You see, catalytic leadership begins with a decision:

• A decision not to sit on the sidelines any longer but to step into the game and take the ball.

• A decision to do the reps in practice when no one is watching.

• A decision to eat smart.

• A decision to make sleep discipline a priority.

• A decision to choose what you want *most* rather than what you want *right now*.

John Maxwell notes, "Our decisions, not our conditions, determine our quality of life."

You and I are the product of our choices. Our leadership mindset will determine how far we go, how well we lead, and what the potential is for future growth.

Remember, today is a fresh beginning.

I believe leadership is a skill, and like any skill, it can and should be developed to maximize the results.

I believe you can learn from anybody. (Sometimes you learn what not to do—but that can be helpful too.)

I believe leaders are servants at heart.

I believe the best is yet to come. Our best days have not arrived yet; they're not in the rearview mirror. They are ahead of us.

I believe God has given you and me everything we need to do everything He has called us to do.

I believe growth is possible for anyone *if* you're intentional about it.

In my own leadership journey, I've learned, I've listened, and I've led. I've been a daily practitioner of leadership, both in the business world and in the nonprofit (church) world. I have learned many lessons during that time, many of them the hard way. But my goal has been and ever will be to invest what I've learned into other leaders. I believe God never wastes an experience; everything He allows into our lives can be used not only for our benefit, but also for the benefit of those around us.

In this book, I've attempted to capture and distill some of my learnings from my first three decades in leadership. I know I have much to learn, and I approach each day with that mindset. My goal here is to add value to you, to help you learn how to lead in a way that is truly catalytic.

We live in disruptive times. We are not the first and are not likely the last to do so. But leadership plays an important and unique role in disruptive times. Catalytic leaders can help navigate disruption like few others while causing no small amount of disruption themselves because they are not content with what is. We will not be shackled to mediocrity, to the status quo, to "the way we've always done it." We see beyond the disruption, beyond the present, to what isn't yet, and we lead people toward the future that could be and should be.

Jim Collins, in his book *Great by Choice*, wrote, "When a calamitous event clobbers an industry or the overall economy, companies fall into one of the three categories: those that pull ahead, those that fall behind, and those that die. The disruption itself does not determine your category. You do."[2]

I'll state clearly from the outset that I'm a person of faith. I began my leadership journey in the business world, and I've spent the last twenty-four years serving as a pastor and leader in the local church. Much of what I've learned has been in that context, but I've also learned from small business owners, military leaders, corporate executives, nonprofit leaders, computer programmers and IT professionals, coaches and personal trainers, and financial executives. I've discovered in coaching leaders that leadership principles are transferable, no matter the context. I've been a leadership coach for people in every arena listed above plus more, and the principles we're going to talk about in this book are the principles I've used with them. They worked for them, and they will work for you too.

I chose the name Catalytic Leadership for my company because I believe great leaders are catalytic. The best leaders make things happen. And my goal is to invest what I've been privileged to learn into others, so that every leader can *intentionally* grow and thrive. Growth never happens by accident; we don't wake up one day and think, "Wow, I'm a fully mature and developed leader! How'd that happen?" Growth takes intentionality, and through coaching leaders, writing about leadership, and speaking to leaders, my goal is for leaders to make *intentional* growth a major priority in their lives and leadership.

As I have coached and invested in church, business, nonprofit, and government leaders for nearly thirty years, I've discovered twelve key principles that can apply to you and help you grow intentionally, no matter your field. No matter where you lead, these principles apply and will help you to pursue intentional growth.

Are you ready to learn what makes a catalytic leader? Are you ready to take intentional steps into your own catalytic leadership journey?

Let's get started.

Chapter One

Cultivate a Teachable Spirit

In 2004, when I first came to Southview, where I serve as the lead pastor, I met with the small group Bible study leaders. I wanted to spend the majority of my first months listening to their stories, hearing what mattered to them and where their hearts were. Listening is one of the greatest skills a leader can possess and one that has to be worked on consistently. In that meeting, while listening was my first objective, my second was to communicate what I called the one non-negotiable for leadership on our team. Most any other skill can and should be learned and developed, but the one non-negotiable was one that I could not teach them. They either had it or they didn't.

What is it that I told them was absolutely non-negotiable? A teachable spirit.

Andy Stanley said, "Be a student, not a critic. I never criticize something I don't understand. We naturally resist things we don't understand and can't control. As a leader, you must overcome that tendency. The moment you start criticizing, you stop learning, and then you stop leading."[1] Leaders must have a teachable spirit, a willingness and eagerness to listen and learn.

Teachability begins at the top. If the leader and the senior team don't model it, it will not become part of the organization's DNA. It doesn't happen by accident; it must be cultivated.

The Garden

Cultivation is a word typically used in the context of farming or gardening. To cultivate is to prepare and use land for crops or a garden to grow food. It involves intentional actions to prepare, plant, feed, water, and tend to what is planted.

A few years ago, I decided I wanted to grow a small garden in our backyard. Now, it should be noted that I have never been described as having a green thumb. I have the dubious honor of having killed pretty much any plant I've ever tried to have in my office or home. For something to live, my wife Charlotte has to be the primary caretaker. I'm just not great at that.

But I wanted to try a garden.

You already see what's coming, don't you?

I bought an above-ground container, a box on stilts, for my garden. I researched the proper things to do, and I bought some soil to go into my "garden on stilts." I bought some seeds and researched how far apart to plant them, which of them to plant next to each other (and which not to), and how often to water. I was set.

All that planning and preparation? That's cultivation.

In the case of my "garden," alas, my preparation and cultivation was for naught. Nothing grew. I did not get to enjoy the taste of my own cucumbers, tomatoes, and onions fresh from the soil. I'll just chalk that up to my apparently unbroken record of failing to keep plant life alive.

Like that container, those seeds, and that soil, **a teachable spirit must be cultivated** in the life of every leader—not just once, but continually. That's the first key to catalytic leadership. And when you do that, you will find much more success than I had with my "garden."

Perpetual Optimism

Warren Bennis, in his book *On Becoming a Leader*, notes that "not one good leader lacks optimism, even unwarranted."[2] How can one be optimistic, even without cause to be so? That's one of the fruits of a teachable spirit. It's believing that the best days are ahead, that the best is yet to come, that we're not there yet but we're going to continue moving toward our goal. Optimism, like other emotions, is contagious, and when a leader leads from that place, the team recognizes and resonates with it. Marcus Buckingham wrote, "The opposite of a leader is not a follower; it's a pessimist."[3] One of Colin Powell's principles of leadership was that "perpetual optimism is a force multiplier."[4] An optimistic leader is a force to be reckoned with and can make the difference to the success of a team or organization.

That's not to say the leader should be oblivious to reality though. We have to recognize what reality is, not try to float above it on clouds of ignorance or blindness. Optimism through adversity is a key character development that I see often in leaders. When the chips are down, when the battle is not going well, will you still believe that victory is possible, even eventually? When the leader does, the team can; when the leader doesn't, the team simply won't.

Avoiding the Drift

One of the greatest challenges for any organization is to avoid a drift into mediocrity. It doesn't matter the industry, the field, the size, the location; *any* organization is liable to drift into maintenance mode, where learning, adaptation, and change are not a regular occurrence. When I'm speaking to church leaders, I remind them of the truth that we all know: Excellence honors God and inspires other people, and mediocrity does neither. I coach leaders in all manner of industries, from all organizational sizes, and I've discovered this to be true across the board.

How do you avoid this drift?

Here are five ways I've developed over the years to address this, both in my own leadership and as I coach others in this nonnegotiable, critical element of catalytic leadership. I'll be touching on each of these further in other places in this book, as they are all part of what it means to be a truly catalytic leader.

1. Pre-Decided and Determined Intentionality

A teachable spirit is not something that's just going to appear in your life. I've never once met a leader who grew and matured by accident. It's *always* the result of intentionality.

This is a choice that you and I have to make every day. Will I *choose* to be intentional today about maintaining and growing my teachable spirit? Will I keep my eyes and ears open in every situation I find myself in today? Will I listen for what I can learn, either from the circumstances or from those around me? Will I remember that I can learn something every day, and from anyone—even if it's what not to do?

What is your *intentional* plan to grow in your teachability every day?

For me, this determines the books that I read, the podcasts I listen to, the webinars, conferences, and workshops I attend, and the articles and blog posts I will digest. Every piece I choose to interact with will help develop the leader I am becoming. They will inform and drive my thoughts, and as Craig Groeschel has said, "The direction of your leadership is driven by your thoughts."[5]

What is the direction of your thoughts? What are you ingesting in your mental diet?

We'll touch more on this in Chapter Three as we talk more about intentional growth, but for this part of our discussion, bear in mind that intentionality is a choice that we must make daily.

Remaining teachable over time takes intentionality. It's not just going to happen. Often, as leaders gain experience and knowledge, they become less teachable, preferring to share what they know rather than listening to what others have to say. That's not helpful, and over time, an unteachable leader will find that fewer and fewer people are following and listening to them.

Journalist and TV interviewer Larry King once said something I found so valuable that I wrote it down and have kept it since. "I remind myself every morning: Nothing I say this day will teach me anything. So if I'm going to learn, I must do it by listening. I never learned anything while I was talking."[6]

That's intentional teachability.

Andy Stanley said it this way: "Closed minded leaders close minds. When that happens, your innovators will leave and you will be left with the people who want to maintain the status quo."[7]

I don't know a great leader who would be happy with that.

Focus on intentionality with your teachable spirit.

2. The Environments I'm In

The environments we are in matter *far* more than we think. Is affirmation part of your environment? Are you intentionally choosing to put yourself in places that will challenge you, that will make you think differently, and that will help you grow beyond where you are today?

Environments are often dismissed as irrelevant and overrated, but they are significant. From the physical environment in which we work, to the emotional environment of the team with which we work, to the spiritual environment that we operate in, each of these can affect what we do and how we do it.

Whom do you spend time with? What conferences are you choosing to attend to stretch your leadership? What workshops or seminars are you attending to help you to move from where you are today to where you want to be? What books are you choosing to read to saturate your thoughts? What are the environments like where you spend most of your time? These questions reflect how purposeful you are about the environments you choose to be in.

Growth happens in conducive environments.

When I'm writing, I prefer a low-noise environment. But when I'm planning or strategizing, conversation with others will help bring out the best ideas. Discover how you are wired and what environments bring out the best in you. (See Chapter Two for more on this.) The people around you matter and affect your environment. Your workspace can add to or subtract from your motivation.

Maybe for you it's the temperature in the room, or the decor, or the color of the walls. Maybe it's the volume of ambient noise, or the need for some soft (or loud) music. All of these and more contribute to the environment, and environments always matter.

3. Community: The People Around Me

This is similar to environments above but focuses more on the people we choose to spend time with. Author and speaker Charlie "Tremendous" Jones said, "Five years from now, you will be the same person you are today except for the people you meet and the books you read." The people you spend time with matter. They influence your thinking, your growth, your responses, and your future.

I read once that the average American reads three books (total) after they graduate from high school. Three! That breaks my heart for them. Not every reader is a leader, but one thing I've seen time and time again: every great leader is a reader.

Who are the authors you are learning from these days? And who are the five to ten people that you spend the most time with?

Motivational speaker Jim Rohn once said that "we are the average of the five people we spend the most time with." That's the power of community. The people around you have tremendous influence in your life. Are they optimistic? You will begin to bend that way. Are they focused on what could be? You will begin to get excited about potential and possibility. Conversely, are they pessimistic? You will begin to bend that way too. Are they focused on all the reasons why something won't work? That will begin to be your default thought pattern.

According to social psychologist Dr. David McClelland, "the people you habitually associate with determine as much as 95% of your success or failure in life."[8]

I like to be around other leaders, talking through issues that we struggle with and wrestle through. Being around leaders who are further down the road than I am helps to sharpen my thinking, expand my perspective, and inform areas where I might not be strong. I will invite other leaders to breakfast, coffee, or lunch, and I will bring a few questions and a notebook and pen to capture what I learn.

The people I choose to spend time with are part of the environment I create, and it determines whether I'm growing more teachable or less. Stasis exists only in a laboratory; we're either growing more teachable or less. I want to intentionally choose people for my inner circle who help me grow and become more teachable.

The books I read are from authors I want to learn from. Don't let just anyone speak into your life. Be purposeful and intentional about what you read because you are inviting those authors into your intellectual community. That doesn't mean to read only what you agree with from people you agree with. That's a horrible path; it's a sure-fire way to avoid being stretched by new ideas. I read broadly from a variety of disciplines, but I'm intentional as I choose what I read next, always being mindful to eat the fish, leave the bones.

Whom are you spending time with? Who is in your inner circle? How does your community help you become the best possible version of you?

Put yourself around leaders who are further down the road than you are right now. Spend time with them. Learn from them. Ask questions. Listen to their stories. And see what God teaches you through them.

4. Evaluation and Weekly Review

Many years ago, I instituted a practice that continues to this day.

Every week, I review the past week and plan for my upcoming week. What did I learn? What went right? What went wrong? What decisions would I make differently next time? What can I learn from the conversations I had with team members? How can I better equip and inspire others through my words and actions?

Looking forward, what are the meetings that I have scheduled? What preparation do I need to do, mentally and otherwise, for those meetings so I can bring my best?

As John Maxwell has said, "Asking the right questions is the first step in getting to the right answers."[9] Those questions and others help me to learn from what's happened and to prepare for what's ahead.

Abraham Lincoln once said, "Give me six hours to chop down a tree, and I will spend the first four sharpening the ax." I tell my daughters the old British Army adage all the time: Prior planning and preparation prevents poor performance.

When I am in a difficult season that seems packed with obstacles and adversity, I think about a quote from Michael Hyatt: "What does this season make possible?" Your current season might be difficult. Challenging. No doubt about it, I've experienced seasons like that. No one can foresee the future and tell us exactly what this is going to look like on the other side.

But leaders, I challenge you to think about that sort of season a little differently.

John Maxwell said, "Leaders see more than others see, and they see before others see."[10] Leaders have a different way of looking at the world, and we see a different picture than what others see.

Others see problems.

Leaders see possibilities.

There's another quote in this same vein by Albert Einstein: "In the middle of every difficulty lies opportunity."

It's easy to see your current circumstances as hard. Everyone can do that.

Leaders ask the question above: "What does this season make possible?"

What possibilities exist now that did not before?

What opportunities are now visible?

What new potential is there that I didn't see before?

Evaluate. Review. And ask the right questions.

Warren Bennis, who is considered to be an early pioneer in the field and study of leadership, was once asked what makes great leaders fail. He had three responses:

- The leader could not abandon their ego. The interference of ego is the death of leadership.
- The leader could not adapt to a changing world.
- The leader stopped learning.[11]

May those never be true of you or me. Catalytic leaders never stop learning; that's part of cultivating a teachable spirit.

5. Investing My Learnings into Other Leaders

The best way to learn something is to teach it. When I share what I am learning with others, it drives that learning deeper into my own life. Often, in the process of sharing, another leader will share an insight or ask a question that will make the learning even better and more helpful for me and others.

If leaders don't develop other leaders, new leaders don't get developed. A non-leader does not develop leaders. Again, you can learn from anyone, even from non-leaders or from those you're investing in. But leaders develop leaders; that's just how it works. And when you're developing leaders, don't just talk at them. Listen. You might be surprised what you learn; I certainly have been. Humility is always the choice of champions.

Jim Collins profiled this in his classic book *Good to Great,* and John Dickson traced the history of our cultural valuing of humility in his book *Humilitas.* Humility is a key trait of great leaders. Don't forget Robert Greenleaf's book *Servant Leadership,* published decades ago but still a valuable resource for any leader willing to put this into practice. Dickson defines humility simply as "the noble choice to forgo your status and use your influence and power for the good of others, not yourself."[12]

If you're a follower of Jesus, you know the source of the concept of servant leadership. In Matthew's biography of Jesus, we read, "Jesus called them together and said, 'You know that the rulers of the Gentiles lord it over them, and their high officials exercise authority over them. Not so with you. Instead, whoever wants to become great among you must be your servant, and whoever wants to be first must be your slave —just as the Son of Man did not come to be served, but to serve, and to give his life as a ransom for many'" (Matthew 20:25–28).

"Not so with you." You don't lead by lording your position, your power, or your authority over others; instead, you lead others by serving them.

Investing my learnings into other leaders reminds me of that core principle and helps me to cultivate a teachable spirit.

I Am *For* You

Remember that the next generation of leaders needs someone who has gone before them to be *for* them, to be on their team and invest intentionally, believing the best about and for them. I love how Jeff Henderson writes about this in his book, *Know What You're FOR.* By listening, learning from their insights, and sharing what we have learned, we can demonstrate that we are indeed *for* them, not against or afraid of them.

Every leader needs someone they are investing and pouring into, and that person needs to know that you are *for* them. That doesn't mean you're just blowing sunshine at them all the time with no critical assessment of reality. But it does mean they never doubt that you are in their corner, cheering them on and wanting to see them succeed.

When someone steps into leadership for the first time, they are on a significant learning curve. That's to be expected. But don't make the mistake of thinking you have nothing to share with or invest in other leaders. If you are one step ahead of someone else on the journey, you can share that one step and what you learned with someone else who hasn't taken it yet.

I think many times leaders think they have to wait until they are in their fifties or sixties to invest in and mentor other leaders. Nothing could be further from the truth. If you don't start doing it now, you likely won't do it then. Build this as a habit in your life regularly; it's what catalytic leaders do.

Fearless Truth-Telling

When I worked in Texas, I got to know a guy who's been a friend to me now for over twenty years. He is one of the most direct, honest people I have ever met. And one aspect I value most about him is that he is a fearless truth teller, like the prophet Nathan in ancient Israel. He does not cower to someone's title, authority, power, position, or rank. When invited, he will speak truth into any situation.

I believe every leader needs a fearless truth teller in their life.

It's easy, over time, to surround yourself with people who think you're doing a phenomenal job as a leader. That's nice, isn't it? To receive that kind of affirmation and encouragement? John Ortberg was right when he said, "The higher you rise in an organization, the less truth you are likely to hear. The shadow mission of the organization becomes to appease and please the leader."[13]

But what if those folks have other motives than speaking truth?

Leaders need at least one (preferably several) people in their inner circle who will speak truth to them, honestly and directly. I'm not talking about someone who's a jerk; there's too much of that going around. I'm talking about people who love you, who want the best for you and for the team or organization you lead, and who want to see you grow into the best version of yourself possible. When you find someone like that, you've found a person of tremendous value.

Does that truth sting sometimes? You bet it does. But that's a sting that helps you get better. Remember what King Solomon said, "Wounds from a friend can be trusted, but an enemy multiplies kisses" (Proverbs 27:6). Having someone in our inner circle who can ask the hard questions, who can question our very motives, will help us more than just about anything else. It will protect us from what John Ortberg calls the "shadow side of leadership." I need—and you need—someone who is questioning our motives, because, as Ortberg said well, "We are all a mixed bag of motivations."[14]

Jon Acuff writes, "Leaders who can't be questioned usually end up doing questionable things."[15] Have you seen this? I sure have. In all walks of life, we've seen leaders who crash and burn, who go off the rails because they refuse to be questioned by people (they think are) beneath them.

Feedback from a fearless truth teller can be exactly what a leader needs. But always remember, leaders eat the fish and leave the bones. If you get feedback that is not helpful, that is not accurate, or from someone who is not cheering for you to be the best version of you, then let it fall to the ground and disregard it.

Authenticity and Humility

Most leaders I know would agree that leadership requires ego.

You stand and speak, believing that your words will make a difference. You lead other people, believing that you're leading them toward a necessary goal that will make life better. That requires a certain amount of ego; a mouselike leader doesn't last long.

But there's a big line between appropriate ego (also known as humility) and inappropriate ego (also called egotism).

With egotism, it's all about the leader. Their ideas are always best; their plans are sacrosanct. They know better, and they're not afraid to tell you so. Don't bring your ideas; they're not required. The egotistic leader knows all, except what leadership really is, of course.

Leaders who lead from humility, acknowledging others' skills, gifts, and contributions in an appropriate way and affirming those, are leading from a place of authenticity. And authentic leaders, while rarer than they should be, are the ones we are drawn to and love to work for.

Leaders who lead from a place of inauthenticity, on the other hand, will eventually be found out.

How many times have we seen this in just about every sphere of influence?

• Political leaders who demand obedience to a law or restriction but then decide not to follow it themselves, practicing "one rule for thee, another for me."
• Business leaders who make layoffs and staff reductions par for their course in order to increase profit on the bottom

line but then receive multimillion-dollar bonuses themselves.

• Church leaders who speak out for or against a certain behavior while being inconsistent in their own personal life, engaging in the very behavior they might rail against at the microphone.

• Homeowners Association leaders who demand conformity to the tiniest, most annoying rules while refusing to acknowledge personal rights over the property on which homeowners are paying the mortgage!

Okay, maybe that last one is just in my craw.

Authenticity matters. As Craig Groeschel says often, "People would rather follow a leader who's always real than one who's always right."[16] And Patrick Lencioni echoes the idea, noting that "People will follow a leader into a fire if they are real, honest, and vulnerable."[17]

Leaders, it's time to make a commitment. Drive down that marker deep and commit, "No one will ever be more teachable than I am." Do what it takes to develop this one; you'll never regret it.

Leaders model a teachable spirit. It begins at the top and works its way down through the organization.

—ele—

Chapter Two

Discover Your Wiring

W hy did you become a leader?

I heard Patrick Lencioni say once, "Leaders want to sacrifice themselves for the good of others, even if they don't know if there will be a return on their investment."[1]

When I attended my first leadership conference at the age of fifteen, I realized what an incredible privilege, honor, and responsibility leadership was. By studying the lives of great leaders of history, we were exposed to the power and influence of leadership, both for good and bad. I was blown away by what could happen through a good leader and the dangers that are present through the mindset and actions of a bad one.

Leaders are not satisfied with the way things are—with what *is*. They see what *could be*, and they act boldly to catalyze others to make that potential a reality.

One of my goals in life is to help make things better.

- I want resources to be leveraged to the maximum by individuals and by organizations. Wasted resources drive me crazy.

- I want to see people developed to use their gifts, passions, talents, and skills for the benefit of others, not just themselves.

- In the context in which I lead, I want to see the church focus not just on itself, not just on maintaining what is, but instead on the mission it has: to reach out to those who are not here yet and help connect them with their Heavenly Father who loves them more than they might have ever imagined.

- I'm designed and wired to encourage, equip, and help leaders get better intentionally so they can lead with all diligence like never before.

I know that every person on the planet is intentionally designed, on purpose, for a purpose—every person and every leader.

The second key to catalytic leadership is **discovering how you are designed and wired to lead.**

When a leader discovers how they are designed and wired, they can then lean into that, not trying to be like anyone else but being the best possible version of themselves.

It is normal and natural to admire and emulate other leaders, especially at the beginning of our leadership journey. We see men and women who are powerful leaders, inspiring speakers, insightful writers, and we want to be like them. We want to be used like they are; we want to leverage our gifts for the benefit of others like they do.

I get that. I've been there. I've had the privilege of seeing and learning from so many leaders like that. And the strong temptation, particularly among young or new leaders who are not yet confident in their own footing and gifts, is to just copy what we see and hear. I've even seen some leaders copy the dress of the leaders they admire.

This second element—discovery—is about finding how *you* are designed and wired to lead. And that's not like anyone else.

Think of it this way: when it comes to the leaders you respect, admire, and learn from, God already has one of them; He doesn't need another one. He created one—just *one*—of them, and of you. Only you can be you. You bring gifts, passions, talents, experiences, and skills—and how those are mixed together, in your design, is unique to you. Your contribution is unique to you too.

For example, I'm naturally wired as a change agent with the spiritual gifts of administration, leadership, and teaching. I'm also a natural introvert; that's how I'm designed. That doesn't mean I don't like people—far from it. But it does mean that I do not draw energy from being around people. Crowds don't fire me up and "fill my tank"—solitude does. What does that have to do with leadership? I've had to design intentional spaces in my calendar so that I can "recharge" before or after I have a significant expenditure of energy (i.e., when I'm around a lot of people).

But leaders and pastors aren't supposed to be introverted! At least, that's what I had always thought and believed. I look at the those who lead the field, and they are gregarious, charismatic, extroverted types, right?

Not always. I discovered that many leaders and pastors share my natural introversion, much to my surprise. And it's worth noting that there's no one "right" temperament or wiring for a pastor or any leadership role. That's something I was not taught but that I've observed and learned over time through my own leadership journey.

My gift mix—administration, leadership, and teaching—is also not the most common for pastors and church leaders. But that's okay because I can use my unique gift mix for the benefit of those I serve. I've discovered that God puts you where He does for a purpose; it's not accidental. And as a leader, you can leverage your gifts and experiences to help people wherever you are.

Potential

I came across a quote recently that really resonated with me: "The tragedy of life is often not in our failure, but rather in our complacency; not in our doing too much, but rather in our doing too little; not in our living above our ability, but rather in our living below our capacities."[2]

I was not familiar with the speaker, so I spent some time reading more about this fascinating man. Benjamin Mays was a pastor, college professor, dean, and college president. His most famous student was Martin Luther King Jr. King referred to Dr. Mays as his "spiritual mentor," and he said he saw in Dr. Mays "the ideal of what he wanted a minister to be."[3] Dr. Mays delivered the eulogy at Martin Luther King Jr.'s funeral.[4]

The quote by Dr. Mays above speaks to a common tragedy in the lives of so many: the tragedy of what could have been. Too often, I believe we trade what could be for the comfort and supposed security of what is. How many people, near the ends of their lives, look back with regret over relationships not reconciled, decisions not made, or actions not taken?

I believe unrealized and unacted-upon potential is one of life's great tragedies.

Have you ever had someone comment on your potential? Typically, we speak about teenagers or young adults with that term: "She has so much potential!" "Look at the potential in that guy." "I look forward to seeing what she'll do; with her potential, the sky's the limit."

Now, imagine that same kind of terminology used, but decades later.

"He had so much potential—what happened?" "She was full of potential, but something must have gone wrong." When potential is not realized, it's sad, even tragic, to consider what might have been.

Leaders are not immune to this. Often, after a season of adversity and opposition, a leader's tendency can be to throttle back, to coast and not make too many waves. The tragedy is that when a leader begins to coast in complacency, so do the people they lead. The mission is not advanced, the ball is not moved upfield, and a maintenance mindset begins to take hold. Be careful; once that mindset takes root, it's really tough to dig it out.

I can think back on my own leadership journey and remember times when things were tough, the criticism was flying hard and fast, and the way forward seemed less certain. What do you do in those moments? Throttling back and coasting feels right in the moment, but it's not the way of a leader.

At Southview, I frequently teach on how God has wired us according to our spiritual gifts, our passions, and talents, and if we are serving in the intersection of those, we will find our purpose and fulfillment that will last. As a person of faith, I believe our spiritual gifts are given to us by God for the benefit of others. The question we should ask, concerning our gifts, is how can I use this for others? The apostle Peter wrote about this in his letter to the early church: "Each of you should use whatever gift you have received to serve others, as faithful stewards of God's grace in its various forms" (1 Peter 4:10).

The tragedy is "not in our doing too much, but rather in our doing too little." How often is there a dream in the mind and heart of a leader that goes unseen, unheard, and unrealized? By playing it safe, you create fewer waves, sure, but the tragedy is that the dream is left in the land of potential, and all those who could have benefited from it will not.

Potential unrealized is one of the saddest things I have ever seen. And it happens more than you might think. People bow to fear, to the opinions of others, to a desire for safety and security. And when they do, the potential of what might have been does not come to pass. The dreams of a leader might be significant and impactful, but if they remain in the land of potential, that is devastating.

I don't want to live "below my capacity"; I want to top out! I want to use every gift God has given me for the benefit of others. I don't want to do too little; I want to leverage every moment I can for the work He has designed me to do. I believe when I do that, He is glorified, and I will find the freedom and contentment that come from being who God designed me to be.

I want the same thing for you.

How Are You Wired?

Do you know how you are wired? Have you leveraged tools to help you discover your designed wiring?

There are a number of tools that can help you. I've found value in the Myers-Briggs, the DISC, and various workplace and personality inventories.

Today I primarily use three tools with the leaders I coach: the DISC, the Working Genius, and the CliftonStrengths Assessment. Let's look at each of these.

1. The Maxwell DISC Assessment

This is not a new profile, but it is one that I have found helpful. DISC assessments are behavioral assessment tools based on the 1928 DISC emotional and behavioral theory of psychologist William Moultroup Marston. There are many different assessments using this framework; I utilize the Maxwell DISC Assessment with my coaching clients and with our team and new hires at Southview.

I like how John Maxwell wrote about this:

"The first person we must examine is ourselves. That's the Mirror Principle. If our self-perception is distorted, then our attempts to influence others will be misguided and even manipulative. The first person I must know is myself; this brings self-awareness. The first person I must get along with is myself; this leads to a healthy self-image. The first person to cause me problems is myself; admitting truth yields self-honesty. The first person I must change is myself; this empowering attitude paves the way to self-improvement."[5]

The primary styles in the DISC are:

Dominant, **D**river: This is about 3 percent of the population. Margaret Thatcher and Martin Luther King Jr. would be examples of this style. General characteristics include being direct and decisive, a good problem solver, a risk taker, and a self-starter.

Influencing, **I**nspiring: This is about 11 percent of the population. Lucille Ball and Bono would be examples of this style. General characteristics include being enthusiastic, trusting, optimistic, persuasive, emotional, and impulsive.

Steady, **S**table: This is about 69 percent of the population. Nelson Mandela and Mother Teresa would be examples of this style. General characteristics include being a good listener, possessive, a team player, understanding, and predictable.

Compliant, **C**orrect: This is about 17 percent of the population. Albert Einstein and Mr. Spock would be examples of this style. General characteristics include being analytical, accurate, conscientious, precise, and systematic.

Your individual personality affects every aspect of your life. That's why one of the best things you can do to grow yourself and others is to understand your personality and what naturally drives you. When you recognize your strengths and weaknesses, you are able to give your best as you work with people around you. And learning the personality styles of your team helps you communicate with and lead them better.

Most people are a mix of two or three of these (e.g., a DC or a CS). I profile out as a solid C, which like all the others, has some great strengths as well as some significant weaknesses that I have to be aware of as I lead. If you don't know your DISC profile, contact me, and I can help you discover it and learn how to leverage your strengths to their max while being aware of your weaknesses as you lead.

2. The Working Genius Assessment

Patrick Lencioni and the team at the Table Group have recently published this tool, and I believe this could be one of the most useful and helpful products of this type that I've ever seen. I've encouraged several clients to take this assessment, and they then went on to use it with their own teams. It's quite practical, and once the language is understood, it's easy to incorporate into your workplace's everyday vocabulary.

Get more info at workinggenius.com, watch Patrick Lencioni talk about it in the video, and then take the assessment. I had our team at Southview take it, and we use it now as part of the hiring process in addition to the DISC.

3. The CliftonStrengths (Formerly StrengthsFinder) Assessment

I first took this test in 2001 and then took it again ten years later in 2011. Most assessments like this will help you discover where you are strong and where you are weak; the CliftonStrengths focuses on your strengths, and the words they use are not "typical."

For instance, my number one strength both times I took the test was Input. It's defined this way: "People exceptionally talented in the Input theme have a need to collect and archive. They may accumulate information, ideas, artifacts, or even relationships."[6]

That description fits me to a T! I read voraciously, and I use Evernote to archive articles, quotes, and ideas that I accumulate. I have finally begun getting rid of more than a few books; my shelves can't take any more! It's an outgrowth of that Input strength, and knowing that, I can leverage that strength in how I lead and write.

My second strength was Learner, defined this way: "People exceptionally talented in the Learner theme have a great desire to learn and want to continuously improve. The process of learning, rather than the outcome, excites them."[7]

Yes, indeed; learning is a passion of mine, and I pursue it frequently and vigorously.

This is a worthwhile assessment as you seek to know yourself first and then those you lead. By leaning into your strength zone and the strength zones of your team members, you can maximize your efforts and make sure everyone is contributing at their maximum capacity.

Other Tools

I've been fascinated lately with Kathleen Edelman's temperament assessment tool called "I Said This, You Heard That." It's based on the historical Greek framework of the four temperaments and delves into not only how we are wired but what our greatest needs are based on that wiring. These are the four temperaments.

Sanguines (yellow) speak the language of people and fun. They need approval, acceptance, attention, and affection.

Cholerics (red) speak the language of power and control. They need loyalty, a sense of control, appreciation, and credit for their work.

Phlegmatics (green) speak the language of calm and harmony. They need harmony, a feeling of "with", lack of stress, and respect.

Melancholics (blue) speak the language of perfection and order. They need safety, sensitivity, support, space, and silence.

Check out more at isaidyouheard.study.

Putting Your Wiring to Work

Learning about how you are designed and wired is important, and the tools mentioned above will help you do that. But until you begin to apply what you've learned, it will just be information. I talk at Southview often about "Bible bobble heads"—their heads are full of knowledge, but their bodies never move. That's what we want to avoid.

Think through these questions when you're discerning how to take your next step with this:

•   What are the behavioral tendencies and limitations of my personality style?
•   How does this affect my communication with others?
•   What pitfalls do I need to be aware of and avoid?
•   Now being aware of this information, what are my personal growth areas?

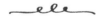

Actively Pursue Intentional Growth

T he third key to catalytic leadership is the **active pursuit of intentional growth.**

While this has some overlap with the teachable spirit we talked about in Chapter One, I've listed it separately as I believe it deserves its own space.

When I began leading as an office manager, I began to ask a lot of questions of my boss, Ron, and his boss, Jeff. Some were operational: "Why do we do this that way?" Some were philosophical, about leadership in general: "Have we ever thought about it this way?" I wanted to learn, and questions helped that process.

When I began working at Bellsouth, I did something similar, peppering my boss, Nancy, and her boss, Bob, with questions. And when I began working in ministry, again I asked as many questions as I could to as many people as I could. I wanted to actively pursue intentional growth. I knew growth was not just going to happen; I had to pursue it.

When I went to work at a large church in Texas, I approached Tommy, the senior pastor, after a Wednesday night Bible study and asked if he would mentor me. He was a bit taken aback, but over the next four years, he and I would meet regularly and discuss leadership and ministry. I learned much from that season. But it began with a request. I knew growth was not just going to happen. I had to go after it, pursue it, if it was going to become a reality.

At that same church, I got to know the senior associate pastor, Jeff, and I found that he was one of the brightest thinkers I had seen. He thought differently and always sought to develop leaders. He invited me, a young seminary student, to join his team at a leadership conference in 2000 that changed my perspective on what the church is and could be. He thought I would benefit, and he gave me a ticket and bought my lunch (always a win for a graduate student). His selflessness and intentionality really impressed me, and his impact on my leadership journey as a whole is really beyond measure. I don't think I would be who I am today if not for him, and I am eternally grateful.

I worked with a team of pastors at that church, and I was forever asking questions and listening in meetings, seeking to learn as much as I could about as much as I could. Did it all apply to me then? Not at all, but you never know when it might. As mentioned in Chapter Two, one of my strengths is Input, and that's on full display when you are actively pursuing intentional growth.

When I moved to northern Virginia to serve at Southview, I began to seek out local pastors and business leaders to learn more about this community and the people there. I have no idea how many breakfasts, coffees, and lunches I had as I sought to learn as much as I could, as quickly as I could. So many people gave freely of their time and advice to this young pastor and leader, and I am indebted to Dee Whitten, Mark

Batterson, Mike Minter, and Mark Seager, just to name a few of the many.

I have always sought to learn from the smartest people I can find. The more I learn, the more I realize I don't know, and the only way to learn is to ask, listen, and observe. Lorne Michaels said, "If you're the smartest person in the room, you're in the wrong room." So true! My goal is always to have people around me who are smarter than I am in areas where they bring value to the team and the organization. My ideas don't always win just because I'm the leader; our goal as a team is for the great and best ideas to win, no matter whose they are. We want to maintain a teachable spirit and posture always.

When our team sits down to brainstorm a new initiative, talk through a problem in the organization, or evaluate something that we just finished, I want people in the room who have different perspectives than I have. I want people in the room who have different gifts, passions, and talents than I have. And I want people who are smarter than I am in areas where they bring the most value. That's how we can best benefit from the diversity of gifts, skills, passions, and experiences that are part of our team. Carey Nieuwhof rightly noted that "yesterday's ideas never attract tomorrow's leaders."[1] I want to continually be growing and thinking forward, not backward. I want to be creative, not historical. Let's learn from the past, sure, but that doesn't mean we live there or try to recreate it, resisting anything new! I encourage our team to think differently, not to be trapped by the way we've always done things but to think beyond the boundaries of the past.

Pursuing intentional growth begins with a learning posture (a teachable spirit). I believe it is so important that it's worth repeating.

Do you regularly choose to lead from and model a learning, teachable posture? Do your team members and those you lead know that pursuing intentional growth is a core value for you as a leader?

Let's get even more specific: what are you learning these days?

Here's an exercise that will bring this home. Grab a sheet of paper or open a new note on your phone or tablet. Write down five things you learned this week.

I'll wait.

How difficult was this for you?

If this was challenging for you, realize that part of your difficulty might be a lack of regular and intentional reflection and processing of what you've learned. That's part of the weekly review process that I mentioned in Chapter One. Setting aside time for active and intentional reflection and processing helps to develop and sustain a growth mindset.

If you are a follower of Jesus, then Romans 12:8 is important for you as a leader. The apostle Paul tells us that if you have the gift of leadership, you are to "lead with all diligence." That means development and improvement, not just resting on your laurels, your natural gifting, or on your past accomplishments. It's choosing intentional growth, now and forever. It's being a perpetual student, seeking to learn everything you can from as many people as you can about as much as you can that will help you lead with all diligence.

You are responsible for your personal leadership development. No one else can be. No one else should be. It's up to you.

I mentioned in Chapter One that my plan for pursuing intentional growth includes the books I read, the podcasts I listen to, the conferences, seminars, and webinars I attend, and the articles and blog posts I digest. It also includes the environments I enter into—the people I spend time with. I have a leadership coach who provides an external perspective when I need to talk through challenges that I face in my own leadership.

I believe every leader needs an intentional growth plan that is designed around their wiring that helps them develop their strengths and leverage their contributions to the team and organization they lead.

The Gift of Disorientation

I love to experience what Craig Groeschel calls, "the gift of disorientation." That's when you encounter a new idea or a new perspective that makes you think, "I've never thought of it that way before." That's the zone where growth happens. If you're not experiencing that regularly, you're not in a high-growth environment. It's time to change that.

The senior pastor I worked for in Texas used to joke that he could tell immediately when I experienced a new idea or perspective. He said I would get a thousand-yard stare-into-the-distance expression on my face and I'd lift my hand to my beard as I thought about what I had just heard. I think I still do that!

Growth doesn't just happen. It didn't just happen for me, and it won't for you either. So how will you determine and choose to grow *intentionally* as a leader? Mark Miller said, "We will not drift to greatness. If we go there, it will be because of discipline and thoughtful actions executed consistently over time."[2] Marcus Buckingham wrote, "As you grow, you become more of who you already are. You grow the most in your areas of greatest strength, not weakness."[3]

When is the last time you received the gift of disorientation? When is the last time you were significantly challenged by a new idea, or knocked out of your comfort zone by something unexpected?

What is your intentional plan for growth?

And what are your next steps toward implementing it?

Like the old saying goes, "failing to plan is planning to fail."

Failure

Speaking of failing . . .

If you've led for any length of time, you've experienced failure. You cannot and will not experience growth without also experiencing failure. The only way not to fail is to do nothing. It's how we deal with failure that matters. John Maxwell said, "Failure should be our teacher, not our undertaker."[4]

I believe that fear of failure is the number one saboteur of your vision and dreams of what could be. Leaders see what could be; they inspire others to imagine what it would be like to get there, to see that, to experience it, to achieve it. But the number one enemy of achieving any goal is being afraid of it failing.

A friend of mine texted me something he heard a few weeks ago: "Many people reduce their life to accommodate their fears." And so it happens. Potential is quashed. Opportunity is lost. What could be, never is.

Fear begins to drive the decision-making process, and the fear of failure causes us to hedge, lower our sights, dream smaller, more "realistically." Seth Godin said, "If failure is not an option, then neither is success."[5]

I remember early on in my leadership journey when I wanted our team to set a specific goal for the following year. We brainstormed, discussed, prayed, strategized; so many words were spoken in meetings and conversations about that process. And, in the end, we set a goal.

And then we didn't even get close to achieving it.

Failure happens. To everyone. Life is not a straight line—up and to the right.

But what if, as Maxwell said, we saw failure as our teacher, not as our undertaker?

Will we allow fear to drive the bus? We get to make that choice.

Thomas Edison, when asked about the thousands of failed attempts as he tried to figure out how to make a light bulb, famously said, "I have not failed. I've just found 10,000 ways that won't work."

That's seeing failure as a teacher, not as an undertaker.

Leaders, you *are* going to experience failure. Maybe this week, or this month, or this quarter. It's normal. But it doesn't have to defeat you or define you. True failure is when you quit trying. Don't make excuses; get back on the horse and try again. Jeff

Immelt, the former president and CEO of General Electric, said, "Excuses turn everybody off. Learn from mistakes and get better."[6]

I think about a question from Jim Collins when I think about failure. Jim asked, "How can you reframe failure as growth, in pursuit of a BHAG (big, hairy, audacious goal)?"[7] In other words, think differently: you're not failing, you're growing! Perspective matters, and catalytic leaders have a different way of looking at failure.

I love Ed Catmull's perspective on this. Ed is the cofounder of Pixar Animation studios and President of Pixar Animation and Disney Animation. He said, "We had to rethink failures and mistakes. Failure is a necessary consequence of trying something new. . . . New ideas are fragile and must be protected, even though at first, they might be off track. We want to make it safe for you to fail. If we do, you will progress faster."[8]

Let failure be your teacher. Change your perspective and learn from it. But keep growing and keep going. Don't let failure demotivate you; press on!

Aja Brown, the former mayor of Compton, said it this way: "It's not that brave leaders never fail; it's that they never quit."[9]

The goal of intentional growth is worth it.

High-Performance Leadership

I don't know a leader in any context—church, business, nonprofit—who wants to be a low-performance leader. We have a limited amount of time, influence, and resources, and we want to make them count. We want to be high-performance leaders. But how do we get there?

For quite a few years now, I've been following the work of the Leap of Reason community. From their website: "The Leap of Reason Initiative is aimed at inspiring and supporting great leaders and funders to build great organizations for greater societal impact. Realizing this mission will require us to influence a mindset change among leaders who play a significant role in the social and public sectors and who are motivated to create meaningful, measurable, and sustainable improvement in the lives of individuals, families, and communities."[10]

The two books they've released, *Leap of Reason* and *Working Hard—And Working Well* have both been excellent reads that led to thought-provoking conversations among different leadership teams I'm part of at Southview. Like any other organization, we have limited resources, limited time, and limited influence. How can we best utilize what has been entrusted to us? How can we know we're making a difference? What metrics are we using to determine what's working and what's not? How can we make a greater impact? All of these discussions have come out of the Leap conversation.

"High-performance organization" is a moniker most organizations—private, public, or nonprofit—would love to earn. And yet who can say what "high performance" really means for mission-based nonprofits? More importantly, how do executives, boards, and funders get there from here?

The Leap Ambassadors Community, a network of nonprofit executives, has spent a year developing clear, actionable answers to those two questions.

In 2015, they released *The Performance Imperative: A Framework for Social Sector Excellence.* It has since been renamed *The Performance Practice.* This is the best work I've seen from them. I don't care if you lead a nonprofit, a business, a church, or any other type of organization or team, this is phenomenal and will really help you frame questions that fit your context and move toward high performance and better leadership. It's only sixteen pages, but it will be of tremendous benefit to you and the teams you lead.

I'm using this to begin and frame discussions with the leadership teams I work with. In it, they define high performance as "the ability to deliver—over a prolonged period of time—meaningful, measurable, and financially sustainable results for the people or causes the organization is in existence to serve."[11] Yes. A thousand times, yes.

The seven core concepts in *The Performance Practice,* or as they refer to them, the seven pillars, begin with number one —"courageous, adaptive executive and board leadership."[12] As John Maxwell has said many times, "Everything rises or falls on leadership."[13]

I strongly encourage you to download *The Performance Practice,* read it, and use it in your team meetings. As a leader, you know that high performance matters. And you know that getting better doesn't just happen—it takes intentionality. This is a tool that can help you get there. You can get your copy for free; check out the list of additional resources at the end of the book.

Reflective Thinking

Do you have time set aside every day to think?

I had never really thought about this intentionally until I heard John Maxwell once say, "Every day I read, I think, I ask questions, I file, and I write." Those are daily disciplines and habits that he has been intentional about developing and repeating until they are a part of who he is.

Part of actively pursuing intentional growth is taking time to think. This involves reflecting on what you've read, heard, or learned. It involves reflecting on yesterday's decisions or conversations. It involves reflecting on what you learned, and what you'd do better next time if given the chance.

"Think time" is tough to come by unless you are very intentional about it. It doesn't feel productive at first. It doesn't look productive to someone from the outside. But there are few things that will help you grow more than intentionally spending time thinking and reflecting on what you are learning. That's how you drive the learning deep; that's how it becomes part of your leadership DNA.

This is a habit I'm developing every day. I spend time reading daily, and I follow that with time just to reflect and process what I've read. Sometimes, I'll jot down a note or a quote from my reading, as well as a statement of what I'm processing in the "slow cooker" of my mind. By writing it down physically with a pen, I find that retention increases significantly. Note this recent research from *ScienceDaily* on March 19, 2021: "A study of Japanese university students and recent graduates has revealed that writing on physical paper can lead to more brain activity when remembering the information an hour later. Researchers say that the unique, complex, spatial, and tactile information associated with writing by hand on physical paper is likely what leads to improved memory."[14]

Screens and keyboards are great. I'm using one right now! But writing manually on paper increases retention, and when it comes to what I'm learning, I want to retain as much of that as possible. So I'll keep my notebook and pen.

Chapter Four

Be Boldly Action-Oriented

L eaders have a bias for action. And that's the core of the
fourth key to catalytic leadership—**be boldly action
oriented.**

Leaders get things done. They do not like sitting and watching
the grass grow. They want to see things get better. They want
to move the ball up the field. They want to advance the
mission of the organization and the team, and they want to see
results. Pastor and author Clay Scroggins said, "Great leaders
want to have the ball when things are hard. Great leaders want
to be the one leading people through—and out of—crisis."[1]

Leading through the COVID-19 pandemic taught me so many
lessons. I've coached and learned from other leaders
throughout this season, and something that has stood out and
continues to grow is the number of leaders who are taking off
the mantle of leadership. They didn't sign up for leading in this
type of environment, and they are weary and burned out.
They've never worked so hard, or seen fewer results from that
work, and that can be terribly discouraging.

I get that. I've felt that too.

This has been an extraordinarily difficult season. None of us have ever led through a pandemic before, with all the government regulations and restrictions, fear, social distancing, and all the rest.

But I'll tell you what I've noticed through this season.

Leaders want the ball.

That's not to say we don't experience down times; we absolutely do. But at the end of the day, when it's time to make the choice whether we will get up again and take another step, we choose to do just that. Len Schlesinger, Harvard professor and President Emeritus of Babson College, said, "If all you do is think, then all you do is think."[2]

Mediocre basketball players don't want the ball. Their fear drives them to avoid aggressively seeking it. "What if I mess up? What if I miss? What if I fail the team?" The incessant voice in your head reminding you of questions like these is not uncommon. But great leaders want the ball. They go after it, believing they can do something with it. Dr. Brené Brown notes, "You can have courage or comfort: you must choose."[3]

I want the ball. I want to take the road of courage. And if you're reading this, I believe you do too.

It's not going to be easy. But no one promised that it would be.

It *will* be worth it.

Do you want the ball? Are you ready to step up and into the future that could be, if only you reach out and intentionally pursue it?

Remember what Hall of Fame hockey player Wayne Gretzky said: "You miss 100% of the shots you don't take."

Get the ball. Take the shot.

What Happens When You Don't Want the Ball?

I can recall times when I did not want the ball, though. When I first came to the church where I currently serve, I came on board as the associate pastor. I remember one question in particular from the interview process: "Do you ever see yourself being a lead pastor?" My resounding response was "absolutely not!" I had a picture in my mind of what skills and personality were required to be successful in that role, and that was not me. I believed, and said, that I was a great "number two," but had no interest in sitting in the lead chair. Too much pressure, and I didn't think I had the right gift mix.

Then, eighteen months after accepting the associate position, the senior pastor left, and the church asked me to consider moving into that role.

I was *not* interested. I had a ton of reasons not to do it, and I could list them, alphabetically if necessary. And yet, the personnel team was persistent, and we agreed to pray through it for six months and see what God led us both to. I entered that season convinced that this was not for me; and I exited that season convinced that this was indeed God's next step for my life. I was not eager for it, and was quite apprehensive, but I accepted it, thinking to myself this would likely be just for a few years. Now, nearly two decades later, I can tell you that on the other side of obedience to God is a sense of peace knowing I did what He asked. It's not been easy, not by a long stretch. But He has been faithful never to leave me or forsake me. He's been with me every step of the way.

I did not want this particular ball. But when it became clear that this was the right next step, I took the ball, and we began to play. And I've had a front row seat to see what God can do.

Persistence Wins

Stubbornness gets a bad rap.

I've been called stubborn more than once. I have an idea, a mindset, a belief—and once I do, I tend to hold on to it until I have a reason not to. I listen, I learn, and I adjust as needed, to be sure, but I can also hold fast when I think I've got the right side of an issue or the right solution to a problem.

I like how Tony Dungee put it: "Coach Noll had always told me, 'Being stubborn is a virtue when you're right; it's only a character flaw when you're wrong.'"[4]

Stubbornness though, if taken to an extreme, can reflect a lack of a teachable spirit. If there is compelling reason to change my mind, to consider another point of view, and I refuse to do so? That's not a virtue; that's just annoying.

Persistence is what we do when we are convinced we're moving in the right direction, when we believe that our course is the right one. Persistence wins. Aja Brown, the former Mayor of Compton, said, "Leaders are not necessarily the best and the brightest. They simply do what they believe needs to be done."[5]

I believe it's a lot easier to do a course correction on a plane when it's in motion than when it's stopped on the ground. I want to be in motion and adjust as necessary. Adjusting from a dead stop is a whole lot harder.

Emotion-Driven Decision-Making

Often when I am coaching leaders, we discover that one of their leadership "obstacles" is related to their emotional response to a person or idea. As we explore and talk about that, I will frequently remind them that emotions are not inherently bad. God created us as emotional beings. Dr. Brené Brown notes, "Emotion dictates behavior. We are not thinking beings that sometimes feel; we are emotional beings that sometimes think."[6] Our intentional actions and thoughts need to be behind the steering wheel. Our emotions need to be on the journey with us; they just need to be in the passenger seat. Emotion is a wonderful passenger but a terrible driver.

I've certainly made more than my fair share of emotion-driven decisions in the moment.

I was leading a new initiative in the church that I and the other leaders believed would be a significant point of focus and emphasis for years to come. We were excited about it, and when the time came to present the ideas for affirmation by the church, overwhelmingly, the church responded positively.

After that meeting, I stayed around to answer questions as I typically do. One man came up to me with a terrible attitude and angry expression on his face, accusing me and the other leaders of "hijacking his church and changing everything." Very calmly, I listened to what he was saying and began to address each of his points, one at a time, in a logical way. He was having none of it. He continued to raise his voice and speak in a most unkind way, and then he attacked my intelligence, suggesting that I wasn't reading the Bible, in his view, correctly.

That hit a nerve.

Unwisely, very emotionally, I responded to what he said with a quick retort that shut him up. That ended the conversation. And since that night, I've reflected and considered my action, and realized that my actions and words were based on emotion. I did not lead well in that moment. And that was the last conversation he and I had. He left the church and never responded to my attempts to contact him.

Why did I respond like I did? What he said hit an emotional nerve, and I reacted. When leaders are reactive instead of being proactive, the results are often regrettable. We speak and act based on our emotions in the moment, the circumstances at that point in time, and that's not the best way to lead. The Hebrew prophet Jeremiah commented, "The heart is deceitful above all things and beyond cure. Who can understand it?" (Jeremiah 17:9). And I have learned that to be so, so true.

As I said before, emotion is a wonderful passenger but a terrible driver.

Think through some of the worst decisions you have made in your past. What drove those decisions? Why did you make them? I'll bet emotion played a significant role. That's why they make terrible drivers; they're only focused on themselves. It could be anger, or frustration, or even boredom. I like how John Ortberg put it: "A low tolerance for boredom does not constitute a leadership strategy."[7]

That is so true. But I bet we can all think of instances where we saw a bored leader hit the gas on an initiative or decision; perhaps you've seen or even been guilty of that.

Bold Financial Moves

Let's talk about some examples of bold action with regard to finances.

When I came to Southview, the church was nearly a million dollars in debt. And it was old debt; a decades old mortgage that kept getting refinanced to keep the payment low (and the debt big). Nearly 70 percent of the budget was going to personnel, a fixed cost that doesn't flex (unless you lay people off or they leave). Financially, there were almost no cash reserves to speak of.

It was a mess.

To be fair, this was normal, just like it is for many, many churches and organizations. Survival mode was what they knew. It had been that way for years. Trying to survive, as many churches do, means anything beyond that is seen as a luxury, something we hope we'll be able to do one day. But hope is not a strategy.

I remember getting a good look at the overall picture and realizing that unless something changed, nothing would ever change. The future was hamstrung by decisions made in the past.

I sat down with one of our volunteer leaders who served as the church's treasurer. I explained what I saw, and he agreed with my assessment. Then I told him, "We've got to pay this mortgage off and build reserves. That's the only way we're going to be able to move forward into a place of health financially. We're limiting our future because of this."

Together, we put together a plan to pay off the mortgage in seven years.

That was a really big, hairy audacious goal—a Jim Collins-worthy bold BHAG—for a church that had never really thought it would be possible in anywhere near that time frame.

It involved committing a very large portion of our annual budget, nearly 30 percent at first, to that single goal.

That was crazy!

But how important is it that we don't limit our future? Mortgaging the future to pay for surviving in the present might seem like the only way to make it, but it is almost invariably a mistake.

And so, we began 2007 with that clear goal in mind.

SCRAM Goals

I will often teach leaders about SCRAM goals:

- **S**pecific: Is the goal clearly defined with a time/date/deadline?
- **C**hallenging: Is this goal going to stretch you in a healthy way?
- **R**ealistic: Are you being honest that this is possible, given obstacles that you cannot change?
- **A**ttainable: Can your team clearly achieve this goal?
- **M**easurable: Will you know when this goal is accomplished and where you are along the way?

The mortgage payoff was a SCRAM goal. We checked the boxes. It would be challenging, no doubt, to earmark that much of the budget. But it would be for a season, not forever. And the positive on the other side of paying it off was that we would be able to free that money up for ministry instead of throwing it away on interest to the bank.

We worked and scrimped to make it happen. We had a lot of things "come up" in those first few years, and we tackled them one at a time.

In 2008–2009, our Elder Board spent a great deal of time praying, discussing, brainstorming, and strategizing about the vision for our church. Every church has the same mission, but every church has a unique contribution to that mission, based on the people who attend and their gifts, skills, passions, and talents. At the end of that season of prayer, we had a clear vision in mind, and we knew that several specific things needed to happen to get us ready for the next chapter of organizational life.

First was a name change and rebranding—a new vision meant a new name, and starting from the name down, the creation of the new culture that we believed God was calling us toward. Second involved some facility renovations to enable us to leverage the space we had in better ways, integrating technology and providing opportunities for hosting learning and growth events. The cost of all that would be about $100,000.

But the mortgage wasn't paid off yet. We were still four-plus years away from that.

What to do? Do we slow down one goal to achieve another?

We prayed and discussed, and ultimately, I went to the congregation with our plan. I told them, "This is what we believe the next steps are. We're committed and ready to move out. And this is what it's going to take to do that. We're going to ask you to affirm this, and then we're going to invite you to help fund it and be part of the next chapter in this church's ministry. We're not going to slow down the mortgage payoff because we believe that is critical to our future. This next chapter will be funded by gifts above and beyond our regular giving, not by our budget. When we have the funds in hand for each piece, we'll move forward."

After months of meetings and discussion with individuals, families, and small groups, the church overwhelmingly affirmed moving forward with the plan from the Elders. And then we invited people to give to see it happen. And they did. We raised the $100K in about ninety days, without slowing down the mortgage payoff at all.

Only God.

And less than three years later, in January 2013, Southview would pay off that mortgage eleven months early.

It all started with a goal, a realization that what was could not continue. It required change. And that change required intentionality, hard work, sacrifice, discipline, and dedication.

We finished the renovation work in the fall of 2010 and began moving forward. We saw a lot of positive fruit from the investments and decisions we had made. But it was not just "up and to the right." That's not how leadership works.

It would take another decade to get our next two goals accomplished—funding our cash reserves (25 percent of our annual budget) and creating a capital expense (sinking) fund to handle the large expenses that are part of owning property (things like planning for a new roof, resurfacing the parking lot, and renovating bathrooms, just to name a few). By sharing our facility with a church plant that had been renting a school and other office space in order for them to meet and function, we generated rental income for the church that funded the capital expense account without having to utilize budget funds.

Sometimes you have to think differently about the goals and about how to achieve them. I learned so much about this from Dee Whitten, one of my mentors in ministry and a phenomenal leader. Leadership is almost never a straight line, and it's almost never one person who has all the ideas. Our Elder Board team makes decisions together, just as our staff team does. And we find that when we do, our decisions are stronger and more well thought out. We get to leverage the gifts, passions, skills, and experience of all the people around the table, not just one. And everyone benefits when we do that.

The COVID-19 Pandemic

In March of 2020, the entire world was affected by the COVID-19 pandemic. Like so many others, our church stopped holding in-person services and moved online. And like so many other organizations, our team began to meet (via Zoom) and discuss a plan. "What do we do first? What's the best plan when we don't know what's ahead or how long this will last?"

Operational planning is one of the ways I have found to deal with the myriad things that want my attention as a leader. By whiteboarding (or legal-padding, in my home office), I generate best-case and worst-case scenarios and look at the pros and cons of moving forward with proposed action steps.

As we realized that this was not going to be just a couple of weeks, the first thing we decided was to immediately cut any unnecessary expenses.

In crisis, leaders and teams have to prioritize and be honest about it. We used three lists. We asked, "If we lost 50 percent of our revenue tomorrow, what would be the first things we would stop doing/shut off?" That's list one. Then ask, "If it continued, what would be the next things we would stop doing/shut off?" That's list two. And then ask, "What are the things we would never want to touch? What are the core parts of who we are and what we do?" That's list three.

We determined that our staff team was critical to this season, as we needed to pivot into this new reality and make a lot of changes to how to accomplish what we do. From creating an online campus, to moving our small groups online, to equipping and training our small group leaders and ministry leaders, to amping up our ministry to people who were hurting in our community, you need leaders. So, staff costs were on list three.

On lists one and two, we put things like moving lawn maintenance to one cut every two, three, or four weeks; reducing janitorial cleaning and trash removal; cutting all non-essential spending by staff and ministry leaders. If the building's not getting used, let's reduce or eliminate what we can for now until we get a clear sense of what's next.

We didn't have time to socialize these decisions. This was a time to clearly and ruthlessly evaluate, to take bold, decisive action. And we did.

Over time, we saw that financial generosity toward our mission did not drop as precariously as we had initially thought it might. What was the result?

Margin.

We then had the margin to tackle the initiatives and generosity for people and partner organizations that were so needed during the pandemic. We made sure our cash reserves were fully funded, and we prayed, prepared, served, and loved on people in the name of Jesus. Because of margin, fear was reduced significantly, and that freed up our team and leaders to do what needed to be done.

Margin gives you more confidence and freedom to be boldly action oriented. A lack of margin tends to increase the fear factor, and that can cause us to make terrible decisions in the moment.

Catalytic leaders know the value of being boldly action oriented. If we just sit around and wait for someone else to do something, for someone else to lead, we might be waiting a long time. We have been given the leadership gift for a reason, for a purpose, in this season.

Chapter Five

Choose to Be Family-Focused

This chapter is going to apply if you are married, want to be married one day, have kids, or want to have kids one day. If none of those apply, skip on ahead. But think carefully and consider your team members, not just yourself. Understanding this key will help you understand and lead family-focused team members more effectively.

The fifth key to catalytic leadership is to **choose to be family focused.**

Why on earth am I talking about family in a leadership book? What does family have to do with work? Aren't those two completely separate compartments of our lives? One has nothing to do with the other, right?

If that's what you're thinking, then you should know that your thoughts sound like a true descendant of the ancient Greeks.

It is from the ancient Greeks, from Hellenism that spawned from Alexander the Great's conquest of so much of the world, that we get this idea—that life can be compartmented, that one part has no influence or impact on another part.

It's like those plates we get to use at Thanksgiving. They are my favorites ones, with the compartments for your food. Each compartment has a little wall, dividing it from the other foods. I love those. I know, I know, all the food gets mixed in your stomach after you eat it. But that's after I eat it. While I am eating, I want to taste and savor each food's unique flavor. I don't want it all mashed together before I eat it. You might as well put it into a blender.

Many people think of their lives like that plate. There are these little walls that separate one part from another, and what happens on one side of the wall doesn't affect what's on the other side.

To that, I simply say this: good luck with that.

The Wheel of Life

You and I are created as integrated beings, where one part of our life absolutely affects and touches all the other parts. With my coaching clients, I will often use a tool called the wheel of life. You can see the diagram below.

If you rank each of the sections of your life on a scale from one to ten, with one being the innermost part of the pie piece, and a ten being the outer rim of the pie piece, you will have a graphic depiction of the wheel of your life. After you rank each piece, look at your wheel. What would it be like to drive on that wheel?

Could be a little bumpy, right?

That's what I work with leaders to address—the bumpy parts of the wheel.

And family is most assuredly one of the pie pieces.

I have talked to and worked with leaders for over three decades so far. In every case—in *every case*—what happens at home affects what happens at work. And the reverse is equally true.

We might think that we can isolate trouble in one area from the other. And, for a while, you might be able to appear to do just that. The problem is that trouble leaks from one area into others. The "walls" don't hold. David Allen notes in his classic work *Getting Things Done,* "Often some of the greatest pressures on professionals stem from the personal aspects of their lives that they are letting slip."[1]

Don't get me wrong. You won't be perfect. You won't win everywhere all the time. But great leaders know that leadership excellence involves forward progress.

Acute Pain Points

I remember a man calling my office many years ago because he needed help. We set up a time to meet, and he came into my office and shared that he had just lost his job, his marriage was falling apart, and his kids were distant and disconnected from him. He thought that if he reconnected with God, his faith journey would have an impact in those other areas. I agreed to help him, and we began walking on his journey together.

Not long after that first meeting, he got a new job—a better job. That resolved the financial pressure that he was feeling, and resolving the financial pressure helped his relationship with his wife a bit. Things got better. The pressure point wasn't so urgent. And I haven't seen him since that day.

Did he continue focusing on the faith piece of the pie? Did his commitment in the midst of pain continue once the pain wasn't so acute? I don't know; despite reaching out to him multiple times, I haven't heard from him since.

There are times when the pain will grow so acute that we are willing to do whatever it takes to resolve it. We will begin to talk about and address areas of our wheel that we have ignored, sometimes for decades. But what happens when the wheel starts to ride more smoothly?

The difference for a catalytic leader is they don't stop working on the wheel when it begins to smooth out.

We are created to be integrated beings, with every part aligning with every other. To have integrity is to be integrated, with no outlier parts of our lives that don't match up. Integrity matters for every catalytic leader I know. It matters a great deal to me. And I want to help you have integrity in every part of your life. Family matters.

More Important Than My Marriage?

In the late 1990s and early 2000s, a TV show captivated my attention. To this day, I will still watch old episodes from this series, *The West Wing*. Aaron Sorkin created and wrote many of the episodes, and the writing in particular is what draws me to watch them again and again.

In one of the early episodes, Leo McGarry, who is the chief of staff to the president of the United States, is working late at the office, navigating the hurdles of a particular piece of legislation. He gets home after one in the morning and finds a small box on the table inside the entry of his home. His wife is on the stairs, asking what kept him, and he briefly explains, and then he asks, "What's this box?" She sighs and says that it is an anniversary present for him; it's their wedding anniversary—which he has completely forgotten.

Ouch.

The conversation continues, and one exchange in particular has been stuck in my memory for over twenty years now. Leo's trying to explain how important his job is and why this legislative bill and this point in time are so important, and she says, "They're not more important than your marriage." Leo replies, "They are more important than my marriage right now.

For these few years, while I'm doing this, they are more important than my marriage right now."

That is striking. It is horrifyingly honest. And it's repeated, sometimes in similar words, in too many leaders' marriages.

Leaders, let me say this as kindly and gently as I know how.

Your job is *not* more important than your marriage. Not now. Not for this season. Not ever.

When I teach and coach on this topic, I will often use a whiteboard and draw four categories for the priorities of a leader:

1. Your relationship with God

2. Your relationship with your spouse

3. Your relationship with your kids

4. Everything else

That's the order. If you're a person of faith, your relationship with God is your first priority. Nothing comes before that.

If you're married, your spouse is your second priority. Only God comes before them in your life.

If you have kids, your kids come next. *Not* second. Your kids are *not* the most important thing in your life, despite having heard that from too many people over the years. That's a misplaced priority if it's true.

And fourth, everything else. That includes your job.

"But I'm working hard to provide for my spouse and kids!"

I get that! But do they know that *they* are your priority and not your job? Do they know that you value your relationship with *them* more? You have to tell them, but more than that, you have to show them. Your actions scream so much louder than your words do.

Do you communicate that you love spending time with them? Do you let them know that you'd rather be with them than at the office?

For kids especially, love is best spelled T-I-M-E. I heard someone say once, "We talk about not being able to spend a large quantity of time with our kids but that we're giving them quality time. There's no such thing as quality time. There's just time." Some of the most memorable moments in my family's life are unscripted, unplanned moments of laughter around the dinner table, playing Liverpool (a great card game) after dinner, or just moments of honest and transparent conversation in the car as we travel to or from an event or activity.

Choose to be family focused.

Your Job Is Temporary

Think about it this way. One day, you will no longer work where you do. You will have moved to another job, another company, another church. You will have retired. You will have died. One day, someone else will do what you do. On that day, how important will your to-do list at work be compared to the family you have?

I have sat by many, many deathbeds as people passed away. I have heard words spoken in joy and anguish, in gratitude and in regret. I have never once heard anyone say they wish they had spent more time at the office. I've never once heard anyone say they wish they had spent less time with their family.

I have heard only the opposite.

The regrets are often centered around family, wishing that days and seasons could be relived, priorities re-examined and reset. It's always sad when I hear those sentiments expressed.

I've heard them so often that today I will often ask leaders, knowing what I have seen at the end of life, what if we made an intentional choice not to have those regrets at the end? What if we chose to write a different story now, on purpose?

Some take me up on it. Some don't.

Some focus on their family relationships, knowing those will outlive any work achievements or accomplishments. Some don't.

Some prioritize their marriage, realizing that their marriage relationship matters more than any other except our relationship with our Heavenly Father. Some don't.

And in that difference, I see what makes a catalytic leader.

I do not want to have those regrets. I do not want to wish that I had spent less time at the office and more time at home. So, I am making intentional choices, today, about this. Your kids will not be the age they are forever. At some point, they will move out: to college, to serve in the military, to get a job and begin the next chapter of their lives. That's normal, expected, and exciting! But how much more exciting will it be if we choose to spend time with them and don't carry forward regrets about the time we could have?

Over the last decade, I've noticed a trend in divorces in America. In the past, many divorces happened in the first five or so years of marriage. Marriage is hard work! Melding two lives together, becoming one in marriage, can be incredibly challenging because it requires humility and a giving spirit of mutual submission by both parties. I've noticed in recent years, though, that divorces are becoming more frequent after a couple has been married for twenty to twenty-five years. What happens in that season that is the catalyst for such a momentous, life-altering decision?

The kids move out.

I've heard it too many times to think it's isolated. When the kids are gone, and there are no more basketball games to drive them to, or school events to chaperone, or after-school activities to provide taxicab service to and from, then what? The couple finds themselves at the breakfast table, looking across the table at someone they barely know. So much revolved around the kids for so long. Now what?

This is why I teach that the best gift you can give your kids is not the latest technology, the newest iPhone, or the hottest clothes. The best gift you can give your kids is a healthy marriage. You want them to have one of those, right? They will learn what it looks like, and how to find the right person to build it with, by watching *your* marriage.

Don't end your life with regrets on this. Your marriage matters, and its success or failure will affect your leadership.

Family First?

If we were sitting across from one another in a coaching session, you might be looking at me with a rather incredulous expression at this point.

"Seriously? My family should come before my job? We'll be living out of our car in no time!"

I have heard variations on that theme more than a few times over the years.

How can you lead well without neglecting your family?

Having coached and worked with leaders from all industries, I can share with you that this is not a problem unique to *any* one industry. Leaders of all kinds struggle with this tension—from high-powered corporate lawyers to pastors, from teachers to delivery drivers, from business owners and founders to government employees. This tension is real, and it's nearly universal. So how does a catalytic leader deal with it?

Here's how I talk about this. When there is a conflict between family and work, family first.

That sounds like a hard and fast rule, and of course, it's not. There are always gradations of gray. But that's where communication matters.

Every weekend, my wife and I have our "weekly meeting," where we look at the calendar for the upcoming week and determine who's doing what, going where, and taking care of transporting the kids when and where. That planning and coordination meeting is critical because it is a regular opportunity for honest and open communication about margin, schedule and time constraints, and priorities. It's not her favorite time because that's not her natural wiring, but we both know how important it is.

Here's what I've discovered, based on my own experience and on that of the leaders I've worked with: if you wait until the day of to make the right decision, your decision will often be made based on the feelings and circumstances in that moment, not on your long-term priorities.

By discussing ahead of time and planning, we determine what's important. My wife knows that our family is very important to me and I've shown her that I'm going to prioritize time with her and our girls. I also work, and through that, provide for our family. Both matter. And when there's a conflict, we talk it through with our priorities in mind. What matters doesn't change. But with communication, there's no guessing or assuming. There's no "making a story up in your head to fill in the gaps,"[2] like Dr. Brené Brown talks about. There are no gaps. Clear communication is key. We'll talk more about the importance of clear communication for a leader in Chapter Ten, but realize that in family life, this matters perhaps far more than you ever thought.

Do you have a weekly meeting where you review and talk through what's ahead? Where you make clear priorities and decisions based on what matters most?

Try it out and see how helpful clarity can really be.

Little Eyes Are Watching

For parents, this goes beyond the practical implications I've described above. This moves into the realm of the story you are telling and communicating through your words and actions to your kids.

It's often said that kids will act and model their lives based on what their parents do, not just what they say. If that's true, and I believe it is, then the priorities we set as leaders through our actions will be observed and (gulp) repeated by our kids. Our decisions affect more than just us; our kids are watching, listening, and building their life patterns based on what they're seeing and hearing.

Andy Stanley writes, "The decisions we make today determine the stories we tell tomorrow."[3]

What is the story you want your kids to tell about Mom or Dad when they are no longer at home? What will be the priorities they see lived out in you and the decisions you make?

The decisions you make will determine the story they tell.

You and I are writing our story with every choice, every priority, every decision that we make. Our kids are reading, watching, and hearing that story, and either replicating it whole, replicating it with adjustments (not necessarily the ones we would make!), or determining that they want to reject what they see and hear completely. I've seen and experienced all three.

What's the story you're telling with the decisions you're making?

Catalytic leaders choose to be family focused because they want to be intentional about the story they are writing. They want to be intentional about the story that their kids will tell.

They choose in advance to be purposeful about the priorities that they set and model for their kids. Little eyes (and teenage eyes, and young adult eyes) are watching and learning.

What Matters Most

In the spring of 2019, our older daughter Erin began to have some headaches. They were persistent and quite painful, and despite taking pain medicine and going to the doctor, nothing would ease them. We thought it might be that she was developing migraines, something I started experiencing when I was about her age. When vomiting was added to her symptoms, we determined that a return trip to the doctor was the next step, and after a number of tests, we discovered that she had a brain tumor that was pressing on the back right side of her brain. It was completely unexpected, and not on our calendar of plans at all. She had surgery two days after the tumor was discovered, and the pediatric neurosurgeon did a fantastic job of resecting the tumor, believing that he got all of it.

This began a season in our family's life that none of us saw coming, but that we had no choice but to walk through. And so, day by day, we did. After several weeks of testing, analysis, and waiting, we learned that the tumor was a very rare form of cancer that only affects about fifty teenagers a year in the world. We worked with her oncology team to put together a plan for treatment; after surgery, she had thirty rounds of proton therapy radiation in Baltimore, about two hours from our home. We temporarily relocated to the Ronald McDonald House there for her treatment, coming home most weekends to do laundry and take care of the essentials.

The radiation scans would take less than an hour each day, so we tried to find ways to fill the rest of our days in Baltimore. Visits to the Babe Ruth Museum, to find new places to eat, and numerous trips to the multi-story bookstore (Erin's favorite) were fun. The Ronald McDonald House was fantastic, and even got us tickets to the aquarium one day. Erin enjoyed her first Major League Baseball game to see the Baltimore Orioles play. She would get tired more easily during this, so naps or just resting and reading were also big components of those days. We finished up just before the Fourth of July and were all thrilled to be at the end of that season and return home.

Following her radiation, we began doing MRI scans every three months to see if the cancer was regrowing. For the first five years, the odds of regrowth are about 50 percent. After five years, that drops. We're over two and half years out, and there's been no regrowth seen; we're so grateful to God for that. She now has scans every six months, and we'll continue to monitor her to ensure that any regrowth can be treated quickly and decisively. If we hit ten years without any regrowth, her oncologist said that we won't have to do more scans, as she will officially be on the other side of this.

I share this story with you to make this point: during the three and a half months when we had her surgery, a multitude of doctor visits, and a temporary relocation to Baltimore for her radiation therapy, my mind was not focused on what I was leading at work. I wasn't thinking about our strategic plan, our tactical execution, or who was doing what by when. I didn't completely check out, but as you might imagine, my focus was with my daughter and my family—on what matters most.

I had a team at work that stepped up and made sure things were moving forward. I would check in and was available to them, but our staff and Elder Board made sure I knew that my priority was my family. These leaders made sure that the work and mission of our church continued, that people were served and ministered to in my absence. And so, so many people rallied around us, praying for Erin and our family, sharing resources to help us navigate the unfamiliar world of childhood oncology, and helping to shoulder the leadership load during a season when I could not fully do so.

Leaders, you have a team that you are investing in daily. Hopefully you will never experience what our family did in your life, but regardless of whether you do or not, you can begin now to make your priorities clear and to invest in your team so that they know their priorities clearly as well. When that kind of clarity exists in a team or an organization, you'll be surprised at how positively that affects the work environment and spirit.

People today are looking for a sustainable pace that honors them as individuals who have more components of their lives than just work. When teams and employers understand that and acknowledge family as a critical piece of the puzzle, it makes a significant difference in the work-life balance for team members.

Choosing to be family focused is a decision each person has to make; the team or organization can't make it for everyone. But the leader sets the tone, and you can make it clear that your priorities are set that way and that it's okay for theirs to be too. Communicate with your words and actions that it's even more than okay; it's respected and honored.

That is catalytic.

Chapter Six

Evaluate Ruthlessly

M ark Miller said, "Improvement is impossible if you do what you've always done. Progress always requires change."[1]

Change is not optional for growth; it's absolutely required. But how do you know what change is needed?

Evaluation.

Evaluation is critical to ongoing learning and success. I say this so often that my team can finish it with me before I get to the end: "Experience doesn't make you better; evaluated experience makes you better."

The sixth key to catalytic leadership is to **evaluate ruthlessly**.

Too many people look at resume entries and assume evaluation is part of everyone's learning process. "Well, they've got twelve years of experience in this field, or in this position." Not necessarily! This person might just have one year's experience repeated twelve times, learning next to nothing along the way but just repeating the same things again and again.

Real, honest, ruthless evaluation is the only way we get better.

Football coaches know this. It's why they set up time each week to review video footage of the previous week's game, analyzing the great plays, the errors, and what to focus on in that week's practices. They can also evaluate the other team through video, looking for weaknesses and points where they can capitalize on a hole in their defense or a weak offensive play.

Military leaders know this. It's why they do a "hot wash" after an exercise, talking through what they learned, what they can do better the next time, and why they failed where they did. When lives are at stake, evaluated learning takes on a new significance and importance.

Effective business leaders know this too. It's why some meetings will be devoted to evaluating the last quarter or the last year's results. Where do resources need to be tasked? Where do we need to allocate our best talent, our biggest financial investment, and our most strategic thinkers? Only with thoughtful and thorough evaluation can those questions be answered wisely.

After every event our team does, we ask three questions:

1. What went right?

2. What went wrong?

3. How do we make it better next time?

I learned this model of evaluation from Andy Stanley, who is in my opinion one of the greatest leaders and communicators of our day. He has mentored me through his books, talks, and podcast from afar for many years. This evaluation model has served me and our team well for many years, and I highly recommend it to you. Andy's monthly leadership podcast is a must-listen for me. (See the additional resources section at the end of this book for other podcasts, books, and conferences that I've found helpful in my own leadership journey.)

It doesn't matter if it's a weekend service, a kids outreach event, a community block party, or even a brainstorming session. We can and should take every opportunity we can to reflect and learn from every experience. Evaluation is the way we do that.

What Went Right?

No one and no thing is immune to evaluation. If evaluation is how we get better, why on Earth would we not seek out every way we can to accomplish that? I actively seek out feedback on talks that I give and sermons that I preach. Why? What's the value in hearing people's opinions? Because feedback and evaluation can help me get better at what I do and how I do it. And getting better means I make a greater contribution to the team, to the organization, and to accomplishing the mission. Who wouldn't want that?

We begin with what went right. This is our chance to celebrate the wins! Where did we see the results that we had planned for? Where did we see positive results? Where did we see people step into what we invited them to be a part of?

It's important to start here because celebration is easy to skip. But leaders know it is critical to motivating the team. Celebrating the victories is so important because it clearly identifies what counts and what doesn't.

I love how Andy Stanley talked about this; he said, "What's rewarded is repeated. You have to autopsy success. If you don't know why it's working when it's working, you won't know how to fix it when it breaks."[2]

Celebrate what went right. Celebrate the victories, momentum, and positive movement.

What Went Wrong?

What didn't go right? What happened that we didn't expect or wish had not? What glitches and missteps did we experience?

Don't fall into the trap of thinking that all negative feedback is worthless. Leaders must value and celebrate people who are courageous enough to speak truth. Our online campus director did this for me recently. She mentioned that when I'm speaking for our online recording, I tend to speak differently, making a "pa" sound with my mouth at times between sentences. I had no idea! I was so grateful for her feedback to help me and help us get better, and I told her so more than once. Honest feedback is how we get better.

For best results, evaluation needs to be recorded, not just shared audibly in words. I have a notebook that records what I am currently learning. In addition, I keep articles, quotes, and other ideas in Evernote. It is a rare moment when I don't have in my immediate possession something to write with and something to write on.

It's especially important to capture what happened that you didn't expect. The law of unintended consequences is at play most when you don't see it coming.

Capturing what went wrong helps the team to acknowledge mistakes and admit where more planning or different planning might have made a difference. It demonstrates to the team members that failure isn't a cause for screaming and yelling, and that mistakes aren't swept under the rug and ignored either. What we do matters, and it matters enough to call out and discuss what went wrong and why.

There is a very real trap here of letting ego get in the way of honest evaluation. If a leader is more concerned about appearing bulletproof in front of the team, they're going to push back on any negative feedback that deals with their department or team. You have to deal with this directly and honestly. Evaluation is how we get better, and we have to be willing (all of us) to put our ego in check and the best interests of the team, organization, and mission in first place.

How Do We Make It Better?

Leaders take notes. They record thoughts, notes, moments of inspiration, and ideas. You never know when a great idea will strike. And as Mark Batterson has said well, "The shortest pencil is longer than the longest memory."[3] I've lost too many great ideas because I didn't write them down and couldn't remember them later. One of the things I look for in potential leaders is whether or not they are a note taker in meetings and conversations.

I want our team to get better at what we do. We believe our work matters, and it's worth every effort to get better. And I'll wager that you believe your work matters too.

Asking "How do we make it better next time?" illustrates to the team the principle of continuous improvement. We never settle. We never stop with good enough because "good enough" is never good enough. We aspire to excellence (not perfection), because excellence honors God and inspires other people. Mediocrity does neither.

Capturing the results from this question will help you in future
planning to apply what you learned. Evaluation only helps if it
is applied. Discussion of the evaluation notes as a team helps
to make sure everyone is on the same page regarding what
standards, actions, and practices are determined to be
acceptable and what are determined not to be.

Why Not to Evaluate

There are a lot of reasons not to evaluate:

- You might hurt someone's feelings.
- You might bruise an ego.
- You might say something that someone doesn't want to
hear.
- You might make someone cry.
- You might make someone quit.
- Someone might throw something at you.

All of those are possible if you begin doing this for the first
time. But I can promise you, the benefits of evaluating what
you do *far* outweigh the negatives. Your team will grow
stronger. You will exercise those humility muscles. (See Jim
Collins's work *Good to Great* for the power of humility in
Level 5 leadership). What your team produces will reflect the
effort you put into evaluation.

You and your team will be the better for it. And your team and
organization will benefit.

"How?"

Years ago, I heard Andy Stanley teach on bold leadership. He
said, "Bold leaders refuse to be cowed by 'how.' You can
'how' a great idea to death. Instead, as leaders our response

should be 'wow,' not 'how.' Nobody ever accomplished anything of great significance by stopping at 'how are we going to pay for this?'"[4]

Asking "how" questions is a great way to derail an evaluation or brainstorming session and shut down discussion. It's important, and will be discussed, but never at the birth of an idea. Allow the idea and others like it to be born and tended to for a bit. When you move from brainstorming into planning execution, then you will get to how. You always do. Just don't get there too early and destroy momentum and excitement among your team.

How comes after What. When you decide the proper course of action, the right goal, the next strategic objective, *then* you move to How. But if you put How before What, you might end up somewhere that you didn't want to go, somewhere that is not the right destination based on your organizational priorities and needs. If you let the How details drive the bus, you're likely to miss out on your best What results.

Blind Spots

I heard once years ago that every leader has blind spots; the average leader has three of them. A blind spot could be something that a leader thinks they are great at, but in reality, they are not. The problem with a blind spot is that you are blind to it; you have no idea it exists.

There are a lot of things that I am not great at, and one among many is my sense of style when it comes to decorating or clothing. I simply don't have the gift, the eye, or the sense for it. Left to my own devices, I would wear the same thing every day. My closet would have four or five of the same shirts, and that's what I would wear. My wife, on the other hand, has an innate gift for decor and style. And what she touches reflects that. That's why she buys clothes for us, and I don't. It works so much better that way, and everybody benefits.

So often, you don't know what you don't know. And this is one of the values of having a coach.

Every leader needs a coach who can provide perspective beyond our own and who can ask the questions that we need to hear and consider. It's hard to see the whole picture when you're in the frame; it's hard to get a clear, unbiased sense of your leadership strengths and weaknesses without a coach. That's how we can identify and deal with the blind spots that we all have.

The goal is not to "fix" the areas you're weak in. The goal is to be self-aware enough that you know where your blind spots are, and you can delegate to others who are gifted in those areas. If you have to deal with an area like that yourself, you at least know this is not your primary area of gifting, and you work toward being able to off-load it to someone that is skilled and gifted in that way.

John Maxwell said, "To change means to choose to change."[5] Choosing to engage a leadership coach could be one of the greatest decisions and investments you make to get better as a leader. I know it has made a measurable and significant difference in my own leadership journey.

"We Can't Measure What We Do"

Jim Collins asks, "How do we know if we are improving? What do we mean by great results?"[6]

Too often, I've heard leaders in the social sector of nonprofit organizations and churches say, "Well, ours are spiritual objectives; we can't really measure what we do." I want to be clear, at risk of offending, and quote Jim Collins: "Saying 'we can't measure what we do' is simply a lack of discipline."[7]

Every leader and every organization can ask, Am I getting better today compared to yesterday? Am I moving the ball up the field on the goals and objectives that matter to us? What impact would be lost if our business, church, or organization ceased to exist?

What are the *key* areas that matter most? What are your key performance indicators that you track monthly or quarterly?

At Southview, we focus on five areas that we call the 5 Gs. I first heard these five words from John Ortberg over twenty years ago, and I've found them helpful as we purposefully crafted our discipleship process. Each of these areas has metrics that we look at each month to see if we're seeing movement in the right direction, or if they reflect that we're stalling or declining. This is always a work in progress, and my goal is to adjust these as we discover better ways of learning and measuring. Here are the indicators we currently track monthly, just as an example:

Grace

- How many decisions to follow Jesus did we see this month?
- How many baptisms did we see this month?

Groups

- How many new small groups were started?
- How many total groups do we have currently?

- What is the number of people currently enrolled in a small group?

- How many people attended a small group at least once this month?

- How many new small group attendees did we see this month?

- What percentage of our worship service attendance is in a small group currently?

Growth

- What was our weekly average attendance for preschool, elementary, students, and adults?

- What is our next generation percentage of total attendance?

- How many first-time guests did we welcome this month?

- How many first-time guest households did we welcome this month?

- What was our average online worship attendance?

- How many app downloads did we see this month?

Gifts

- How many new volunteers did we see step into serving others this month (per area and total)?

- What is our current serving percentage of our total weekly attendance average?

Giving

- What is our weekly average giving for this month?

- What is our per capita giving average (adults + students)?

- How many new first-time givers did we have this month?

- How did we end the month financially, positive or negative (income–expenses)?

- How many donor households have we had so far this year?

- How many weeks do we currently have in our cash reserves (goal is a minimum of three months)?

- What is our current staffing ratio (full time equivalent : in-person weekly attendance average)?

Those five G's matter for us because our goal is to inspire people to follow Jesus. We believe that engagement in those 5 G's is the best predictor for an individual's spiritual growth, and we want to see everyone choose intentional growth in their spiritual lives (just like in the rest of their lives). How do we measure if we're doing the right things, at the right time, in the right way that is effectively inspiring and helping people to do that? We measure the metrics above, not just anecdotal stories. Those metrics tell a story every month and over time, and the numbers don't lie.

Your metrics likely will look different unless you have the same mission, model, and strategy we do. But you *must* have metrics that you are looking at, evaluating, and tracking with great regularity. Every month, our Elder Board and staff look at these numbers; they help to affirm movement we see in the right direction and to give us a needed kick to address areas that are not moving the right way. Anecdotal stories can be helpful in some ways, but data-based decision-making is superior, as it removes so much of the emotion that can cloud the process.

David Gergen said, "It is easy in the leadership arena to confuse motion with progress. Busyness is not progress."[8] Boy, isn't that true. I know a lot of organizations that couldn't be busier, but they are not accomplishing their mission. The calendars are full. But is that the metric you want to measure to determine results?

I believe a great question comes from Andy Stanley around this topic of evaluation. Leaders could ask, "What would a truly great, selfless, level 5 leader do in this situation?"[9] There is tension and extraordinary opportunity in that question.

Annual Life Cycle Evaluation

Every year, as we are preparing for our budget season where we plan forward for the next fiscal year, our board does a life cycle evaluation of the different parts of our organization. Every ministry, every idea, every initiative, every organization follows a life cycle. Nothing persists up and to the right forever!

When we do our evaluation, I ask each of our board members to take a blank N curve chart and plot out where they would put each department, event, ministry, and initiative. I first encountered this evaluation method at the Global Leadership Summit in 2011, and it has been an invaluable tool for our team since. Each will fall in one of four quadrants on the chart:

• Accelerating: This area is really getting traction. Things are moving in the right direction; there's passion, purpose, and momentum building.

• Booming: This is right in its stride. This is where we wish every part of our organization lived all the time. It's not perfect, but it's working as designed and contributing to the overall momentum and success of the team and organization.

• Declining: This is past its prime. Something changed— maybe the passion or vision leaked, maybe the need isn't as pressing as it used to be, maybe a leader left and there's no strong leadership there. It's losing steam.

• Tanking: This is dead. We're still doing it for some reason, but it's past time to call time of death on this. There are no results, no fruit, and not much of anything to show for our investment and efforts.

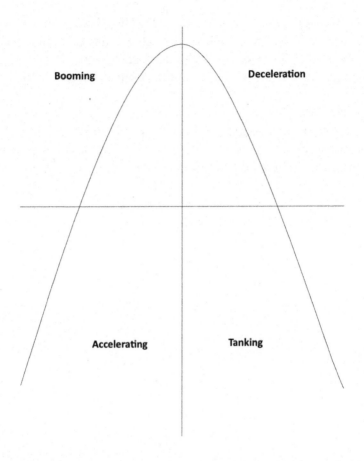

On our own, individually, we put everything on that chart, and then we get together and compare how we rated things. Occasionally there's a slight variation from one person to another, but for the most part, there is pretty amazing consistency, especially on the right side of the chart with declining and tanking. And when there's disagreement, there's often a fantastic discussion around different points of view, which I find energizing and engaging.

This evaluation process helps us spot problems before they drag down the momentum of the organization, and it helps us to address them in a timely fashion, attempting to move them to the other side of the N curve if possible, and shutting them down if not. This informs choices that we make as part of the budget process. "If we retask this position and provide additional funding, could we move that program/department/initiative from decelerating back over to accelerating?" "If we took the resources from what's tanking, which growth engine is showing the most potential right now where we can invest those?"

Many times, leaders can spot things that we need to stop doing because of a loss or lack of momentum or results. But we have to look, we have to ask the right questions, and we have to be willing to act on what we see and learn.

Leaders, our job is to move toward the mess, not ignore it, hoping it will resolve or go away on its own. It almost *never* does.

What Are Your Growth Engines?

Every organization has growth engines—those initiatives, departments, programs, or ideas that are producing far more results than others. Leaders can spot potential growth engines and then reallocate resources based on that potential. Seeing potential is a skill that leaders develop over time; rarely is it inherent, but it must be developed in order to lead toward results.

Have you spent time thinking about what your current and potential growth engines are?

For a church, this might be the family ministry area. Parents care a great deal about their kids, and when a church commits to coming alongside families to invest in their kids, that can create significant momentum and movement. When we help parents get better at parenting, and we help kids grow spiritually, that can be a significant growth engine.

For a business, this might be a product that comes out of research and development around a need that no one else is meeting. By stepping into that space, you are creating a growth engine, one that is designed to address a felt or perceived need by potential or existing customers. That's always a win.

By putting growth engines on your radar, you are choosing to invest in the future, not just the present. You're asking, "What has potential for five or ten years from now?" instead of just reacting to what's working today and trying to continue the same thing over and over. Leaders put their best talent in areas of their greatest potential.

This is one of the reasons I'm not a fan of strict and immovable job descriptions. I want to see leaders and team members grow and thrive, and part of that involves being flexible to move people and resources to areas where potential exists, even if it wasn't present during the last budget planning season. Leaders must be mindful of and watchful for growth engines, and sometimes they don't announce themselves much in advance. We have to remain agile and capable of retasking to wherever potential is.

Chapter Seven

Aspire for Proper Productivity

P roductivity has been a passion of mine for many years
now. For a long time, it was out of necessity. There just
weren't enough hours in the day to get things done. More
responsibility seemed to mean longer, never ending to-do lists.
I would leave the office, not because I got things done on that
day's list but simply because I had to go home, knowing the
list would be there the next morning. Productivity seemed to
be the magic bullet; if I could work smarter, not longer, then I
could get more done and be a better leader.

Is that true?

The seventh key to catalytic leadership is to **aspire for proper
productivity**. But let's begin by defining terms, as productivity
is a concept that is too often ill-defined.

I define it this way: proper productivity involves utilizing the
resources we have as well as we can and honestly measuring
the results and prioritizing based on that data because results
matter.

Have you ever tried to lose weight? Most people can relate to
this at some point in their lives. It's not the easiest thing to do.

Imagine trying to lose weight by eating right—just once a week. And working out—just once a month.

How well do you think that would work?

Probably not that well. And the scale would reflect that. Data tells the story.

Results come from consistent effort over time. Craig Groeschel captures it well: "Systems create behaviors. Behaviors become habits. Habits drive outcomes."[1]

Do you want different outcomes?

You need new habits.

Habits are built from behaviors.

And systems create behaviors.

As a leadership coach, I help clients clarify their goals (desired outcomes) using a primary focus tool. I ask them to write down the four to five areas they want to see movement in during the next six to twelve months. Once we've defined the primary focus areas, then we evaluate current thought patterns, habits, and behaviors, and we begin to design new habits and behaviors to replace the ones that are getting you your current results.

Henry Ford said, "If you always do what you've always done, you'll always get what you've always gotten." Similarly, W. Edwards Deming wrote, "Every system is perfectly designed to get you the results it gets."

To get different results, we have to do different things.

We have to change.

And that's where coaching comes in.

A coach helps you gain self-awareness and perspective. By asking the right questions, a coach can help you discover exactly what needs to change to get the results you want. And a coach can provide the accountability that is part of significant changes in your thoughts, behaviors, and habits.

But it takes consistency. "Once in a while" won't get you there.

I meet with two coaches consistently, each of whom helps me in a different part of my leadership. Over time, those relationships have produced much fruit. But it took time and consistent effort. And I don't think the changes would have happened without the accountability inherent in the coaching relationship.

What are you currently doing "once in a while" that needs to happen every day? What is your plan to change your current habits, behaviors, and systems to get there? Do you have a coach to help you gain clarity and focus and to provide the necessary accountability?

In 1896, an Italian economist from the University of Lausanne named Vilfredo Pareto noted that roughly 80 percent of consequences come from 20 percent of causes. This 80/20 "Pareto Principle" will apply in many areas of your life, but for leaders, I will note that 80 percent of your return will come from 20 percent of your prioritized efforts. When you prioritize well and focus your time and energy on what matters most, you will see a return that is often significantly out of proportion (in a good way). That's the Pareto Principle at work.[2]

Productivity begins with your systems.

Getting Things Done

In 2006, I read a book that would transform the way I operate on a day-to-day basis. It changed the way I think, plan, read, communicate, and meet.

What was that book? *Getting Things Done* by David Allen.

The GTD system and framework are known by many leaders in a variety of settings. From government employees to contractors, from small business owners to corporate executives, GTD has been adopted by millions of leaders around the world. In his book, David unpacks the system and shares a step-by-step process for adopting it, no matter what your industry or what you lead. I recommend this book often to leaders, emphasizing its impact on my own productivity and efficiency.

Are you overwhelmed by the multitude of projects, to-do lists, details, and emails that are part of every leader's life and work? Do you wish there was a system to help you get a handle on things? *Getting Things Done* helped me to do just that, and that's why I recommend it to everyone I can.

Your brain will not efficiently prioritize for you. It will hold getting your oil changed, replying to that email, upping your retirement contribution, picking up the dry cleaning, and going on a date with your spouse all in the inbox of your mind. Each of those has a different priority level—if you prioritize. Your brain simply brings them all up equally, usually at an inopportune time when you can't do anything about them. That's one of the great values of GTD; it's a system that helps you determine what's most important, what should be prioritized, and what generates the highest and greatest return for your goals. Then you create a system that will equip you to execute on every project, every next action, that is needed for successful movement forward.

What generates the greatest return for you? What have you seen the best fruit come from? In business, this might be focusing more on actual income-producing activities versus administration. There's nothing wrong with administration; it's a necessary part of any organization. But that's not going to generate sales, products, content, or new customers.

The more time you spend on doing the wrong things, the less time you have left to spend on what really matters.

No matter what system you use, the fact is you need a system. Whether it's digital or paper based, GTD, or some other framework, an organizational system is a nonnegotiable for a leader who's aspiring for proper productivity.

What a Leader Cannot Do

On a TV show we were watching the other night, I heard a reference to a king I was unfamiliar with, so I Googled him. The king's name was Canute (also known as Canute the Great), an eleventh century Viking warrior who went on to conquer England and rule as king from 1016–1035. He is thought to be the first king to rule over a united England, but he is remembered best for one particular incident in his leadership.[3]

One day, he heard his courtiers were flattering him, saying he was "so great, he could command the tides of the sea to go back." Canute was a Christian, and he knew this was in no way true. So, he had his throne carried to the shore of the sea, where he sat as the tide came in and commanded the waves to halt their advance. They did not.

His point? Though the actions of kings might appear to be great in the minds of people, they are nothing compared to the power of God.

Canute knew something that far too many leaders in our day do not—leaders have limitations. There are things they cannot do.

It is easy (and common) for leaders to begin to read their own headlines, to begin to think that those around you who speak kind words to and about you are telling the whole story. The ego begins to puff up, and once puffed up, it's tough to deflate! Great leaders, though, know what they cannot do. They understand the limits of their power and their ability, and they don't try to pretend to be something they're not.

Leaders, when's the last time you said "I don't know" when someone asked you a question? When's the last time you apologized to a member of your team and said, "I was wrong"? Don't overlook the importance of those simple words; they reflect a heart of humility, and that's critical to great leadership (as Jim Collins has written about extensively in *Good to Great*).

Canute's story was worth reading, and it's a good lesson for those of us who lead, no matter the context.

Assess what you can do, be honest about what you cannot do, and don't try to pretend to be something you're not.

Getting Results

I expect most people who read on the subject of leadership would be familiar with the name Peter Drucker. Drucker was an incredibly prolific writer and speaker on this subject, and he taught more on it than just about anyone else in the twentieth century. From business leaders to nonprofit leaders to church leaders, so many people (including me) have benefited from Drucker's writings, and I'd highly recommend them to you.

Drucker has always fascinated me. He taught so many people in so many different contexts, and seemed equally comfortable in the boardroom, the classroom, and the church meeting room. Did you know that he wrote one-third of his books before age sixty-five and two-thirds after? Often, people think of sixty-five as a magic number, and once you're "retired," you just kick back and stop making contributions to organizations, churches, and the world. Never let that be said! Drucker ran his race to the very end. When he died at the age of ninety-five, he was still writing, working on his next book. I hope and pray that I'm still making a contribution all the way to the end. What a leader.

Here are three of my favorite Drucker quotes for leaders:

1. **"What have you quit doing so that you can focus more on those things that will produce results?"**[4] The principle of planned abandonment is critical for every leader in every organization. Your "stop doing" list needs to be ongoing, regularly reviewed, and systematically implemented. Do less so that you can accomplish more. Stay in your lane; grow in your competency area where you bring the greatest contribution to others and to your organization and mission.

2. **"Thinking small yields small results."**[5] I've seen this to be true more than once in my own leadership. Leaders, let's challenge each other with questions like, "What are you working on that is significant?" "What are you working on that will make a difference?" Think bigger, grander, more significant thoughts. Dream more impactful dreams. Don't limit your future impact and results with small thinking.

3. "Good intentions are not enough; always measure the results of your efforts to make sure you are getting the most out of your investment of time and resources."[6] We measure what's important. Without evaluation, how on earth will we know if we're getting better? See Chapter Six for more on this.

These three quotes can help you no matter your field or industry. But only if you reflect and apply.

What Not to Do

I read pretty broadly on the subject of productivity. And I learn as much as I can from as many people as I can. But as we reflect on aspiring for proper productivity, it's important to reflect on what not to do. I have a plethora of examples on this that might be helpful to you as you reflect on your own leadership journey.

First, realize that you are not good at everything. You're just not! Neither am I. If we are honest, we're good at a couple of things. Marcus Buckingham and others have suggested that leaders would be far better served to focus on our strengths instead of trying to "shore up" our weaknesses.

If I work really hard on an area I'm not good at, I might— might—bring my grade from a D to a C. But I'm never going to be an A player in that area. It's not my natural wiring (see Chapter Two). But if I focus on an area where I'm a B+ or an A-, I can make significant improvement and see that become something very strong.

This can be a very hard lesson to learn.

When I was a new leader, I was constantly battling the urge and desire to want to be good at everything and to focus on everything. I would focus on my work and on the weeds of the work of everyone on my team. And guess what? I was *far* from productive.

I remember early in my leadership journey when I worked as an office manager for a drug store chain. I was responsible for hiring and overseeing about a dozen cashiers and half a dozen or so stock guys. It was my first leadership experience, and boy, was it an eye-opener. Here are a few things I learned about productivity during my two years there:

• ***Busy does not mean productive.*** I can't tell you how many conversations I had with team members who were constantly "busy" but were not doing their jobs. They were in motion but not doing the right things. Instead of focusing on the main things, and on what they were good at, they focused on minutiae that really didn't matter that much. That's a temptation for us all at times.

• ***If you don't deal with a problem, it doesn't go away.*** I had a team member who was consistently late. By consistently, I mean every shift she worked. It was kind of remarkable. How can you be late every time? I talked to her time and again and was reassured each time that this wouldn't happen again. There was always a reason, always a story why it happened this one time. I kept giving chance after chance. And you know what happened? Nothing changed. Her behavior never changed, and ultimately, I had to let her go. But I waited *way* too long to do that. And unfortunately, I've repeated that mistake a few more times since then. It's tough to know when to give more grace and when to hold the line. But productivity really begins with being where you're supposed to be, when you're supposed to be there, doing what you're supposed to be doing.

• ***Doing the right things, day after day, week after week, has a compound effect.*** As I trained and worked with new employees, what I found was that if they were consistent in their efforts, they could almost always grow into valuable members of our team. But if they did the right things only once in a while, they became much less so. Productivity has to mean that you are "producing"—there's fruit from your efforts. No fruit = something needs to change.

- ***Encouragement matters.*** My supervisor at that drug store was a middle-management guy who had risen to the level of a store manager in the company. He wanted to go higher, but he had a number of challenges that seemed to cap his growth. One of those was how he treated his team members. I remember hearing how he talked to and about his team members and thinking even then, "That's just not honoring to them." That wasn't his goal. He saw them as a means to an end—the end being his success, and his next vacation or nice car as fruit for his leadership. In nearly two years of working there, I cannot recall one instance of his encouraging me or another team member. That affected morale, turnover, and productivity, as well as how customers were treated by team members. As they are treated, so will they treat others.

Do Less

One of the most counterintuitive lessons I have learned over the years is the value of doing less.

Yes, I mean doing fewer things.

If you try to focus on everything, you will be successful at almost nothing.

I had a conversation the other day with one of our team members. I shared with her that I'm not really good at what we were talking about. In fact, I'm not good at a lot of things. My strengths lie in three areas consistently over time: administration, leadership, and teaching. Outside of those three areas, I tend to be pretty weak—a C student at best.

Over time, I've discovered that if I stay in my lane and focus on what I have strengths in, I make the best and most effective contributions to our team and our organization overall. When I try to get in the weeds with everyone else, giving my input on decisions that I really don't need to weigh in on, or make decisions that someone else can and should be making, I'm diluting my productivity and maximum contribution. I'm also hindering the growth of other leaders, preventing them from developing their own decision-making and leadership skills.

Remember our definition of proper productivity: proper productivity involves utilizing the resources we have as well as we can, honestly measuring the results, and prioritizing based on them because results matter.

People are resources. Time is a resource. Margin is a resource. Strengths are a resource.

Aspiring for proper productivity means utilizing those resources as well as we can.

That means we do less. And when we do, my experience has been that we are far more effective and make a significantly greater contribution to our team and organizational mission.

Leaders care. Details matter. And that's why it will always be a temptation for us to get in the weeds on things that matter a great deal to us. But disciplined leadership means we predetermine to do less so that we can maximize our efforts and results. It's difficult, but I've learned that it's worth it.

Chapter Eight

Build Up People and Teams

T he eighth key to catalytic leadership is to **build up people and teams.**

People are complicated and messy. And often, leaders can see them as a distraction from the work they have to do. If we could just do what we do without all the messy people, how much easier this would be!

But when we think or say that, we miss a critical part of what leadership is.

In my experience, leaders tend to either lean toward being task focused or people focused.

Meetings

If you haven't read Patrick Lencioni's book *Death by Meeting*, add that to your to-read list. (You do have one of those, right?) Meetings are often bemoaned, seen as a necessary evil. As my friend Wes says, "Meetings are where minutes are kept and hours are lost." I've been in meetings like that; I imagine you might have been too.

What makes meetings such a time killer? Why can they be so messy?

Because they involve people.

We've all heard companies proclaim that their people are their most important assets. By contrast, Jim Collins teaches, "In great companies and organizations, your people are not your most important asset. The *right people* are."[1] They are not a distraction, a nuisance, or a problem; they are the mission. Investing in them is not a tertiary responsibility of a leader; it is a primary responsibility.

Some questions that might be helpful to ask yourself:

- What is the best way I can contribute to the team's success?
- What does my team need from me that only I can bring?
- How can I serve my team members where they are?
- What are the intentional ways I will choose to invest in them this week?

The people you lead are not a distraction from the main thing. They are the main thing.

Shepherding Your Team

In recent years, I've begun having a one-on-one meeting with each of my direct reports every week. Sometimes these are twenty to thirty minutes; sometimes they're a bit longer. The agenda is mostly driven by them; it's a time when they can bring questions, challenges, opportunities, and ideas. We can discuss them, and they have my undivided attention. It's also the time when I can ask them questions like the following:

- What are you learning right now?

- How did that last initiative work? What did you discover? What would you repeat (or not)?

- What are you working on?

- Is there anything you need my input on that's keeping you from moving forward?

- Are you currently running at a sustainable pace? If not, why not?

Over time, as trust is built, we can dive deeper than operational questions:

- What are your greatest struggles or joys in your current role?

- What was your best day at work in the last two to three months? Why?

- What was your worst day at work in the last two to three months? Why?

- If you could do anything, what would you do?

- What role do you see yourself in next?

- How can I help you to develop and grow as a leader to get there?

It's a time I can ask for feedback from them and share feedback with them. That helps our team grow stronger intentionally.

It's also a time when we can discuss (and I can evaluate) if someone is appropriately challenged, under-challenged, or dangerously over-challenged. That's crucial information for every leader to know about their direct reports and senior leaders. It helps us know where to best deploy organizational resources like people, time, and finances.

Through these conversations, I've discovered *far* more about the hopes, dreams, struggles, and expectations of the team members I work with, and I've learned how I can pray for, equip, and encourage them in their current role and beyond. It also helps me discover if their pace is sustainable or if our team is over-demanding of them. I believe that's part of shepherding them well.

Evaluations are then ongoing, not just once a year. Having a once-a-year meeting where you attempt to recall all the good, bad, and ugly for an entire year never made good sense to me. I do evaluations while things are fresh. We provide accountability through our weekly one-on-one meetings. "What are you working on?" "Did you do what you told me you would do when you said you would do it?" This is when excuses begin to go lame; having an excuse every week for why you didn't do what you committed to gets old fast.

Accountability means people will either get things done and improve or leave, but there are never any surprises about performance issues.

Protecting Your Team

How do you respond when one of your team members is attacked or treated poorly?

I remember when my administrative assistant at the time was contacting the bank our church used for our accounts. We'd been customers of that bank for several decades, and while I didn't deal with them directly, I had been under the impression that their service was good and solid.

Was I ever wrong.

I asked one day for some information from the bank, and my assistant called over to talk with someone. How she was treated was beyond unacceptable. We weren't asking for special treatment, but we were treated as a bother, not as a valued customer. They were not helpful, and when I found that out, I called to speak with the branch manager. That too was not a stellar customer service experience. We stopped doing business with that bank shortly thereafter.

As the point leader, I know that arrows and bullets come with the territory. The guy up front is the one often perceived as wearing the bullseye shirt. It's a part of leadership. But coming after my team is a different story altogether.

I don't pretend to always get this right. I've grown a lot from when I was younger, and I've made more than my share of mistakes that I wish I could take back. But my goal and hope is always that anyone who has ever worked on a team I've led would agree that they were treated with respect, dignity, and value during their time on our team. That's part of what it means for a leader to remain people and team focused.

If your team members don't believe that you as their leader have their backs, that is a significant problem that *will* cause cascading problems. The job of a leader, like that of a shepherd, is to protect your team as they carry out the mission.

Encouragement

As I write this in 2021, the United States is currently undergoing a season that's being called "The Great Resignation." People are leaving their jobs at an unprecedented rate. One of the reasons I believe people are so willing and eager to change jobs is a lack of encouragement. Truett Cathy, the founder of Chick-fil-A, said, "How do you know if a man or woman needs encouragement? If they are breathing."

To encourage someone is to "put courage into" them. Tim Elmore has said, "Encouragement is the oxygen of the soul. Interaction is what polishes our character. Relationships are what give our lives meaning."[2] I think he's spot on; encouragement is like oxygen to our soul. What happens when encouragement is absent? It's like running out of oxygen—not good.

Some leaders I talk to think that encouragement is completely unnecessary.

"We pay them; that's all the encouragement they need."

"A steady job is encouragement enough."

"Your encouragement should come from a job well done."

I'm going to respectfully disagree.

I believe encouraging the members of your team is something that costs a leader practically nothing but has inestimable benefits. You as the leader can be and should be the CEO—the Chief Encouragement Officer.

Encouragement is something that I've had to work on over the years, and I've watched what happens when it's present and when it's not. The difference is stark. It's a key indicator of great leadership. John Maxwell notes, "Encouragement is 51% of leadership."[3] I've found that to be quite true.

It's easy to criticize. Anyone can find fault. That's not a gift. But encouragement will take you *much* farther than endless harping. What you reward—what you encourage—will often continue and increase. If you want a certain behavior to continue, call it out! Celebrate it! Mention it clearly and praise it effusively.

Leaders, my challenge to you is to give this a shot. Try planning ahead of time and intentionally speaking words of encouragement to your team members. See what happens. Measure the results.

Do you *really* need to encourage others?

Only if you want your team to stick around.

Only if you're interested in high performance.

Only if you want to make a difference.

Are you grateful for your team members? When is the last time you told them?

Too many leaders are like the husband who, when asked when was the last time he told his wife he loved her, said, "I told her when we got married; if I change my mind, I'll let her know." That's not how marriage (or leadership) works. Gratitude—real gratitude—is never silent or invisible. If it's real, it is always expressed, and it is expressed frequently, with honesty and authenticity.

Do your team members know that you are *for* them? Do you tell them and reinforce your words with actions regularly?

Remember that people join organizations; they leave leaders and managers. They will forget many of the things you said to them and did for them, but they will never forget how you made them feel. That's a key element of your culture. Your organizational culture matters, and it will only ever be as healthy as the senior leader wants it to be.

In the average Christian organization, only 54 percent of employees are engaged and excited about their work. Outside those organizations, in the United States that number drops to 30 percent; internationally, it's even lower at 15 percent.[4] Is that good enough for you? It's not for me. I want every member of our team to be engaged at the highest level. I want them to be excited about their work. I want them to look forward to the contribution they make. When people are serving out of passion, purpose, and their gifting, then they will talk about what they "get to" do, not what they "have to" do. The difference in those two phrases makes all the difference, and leading a team who gets that is part of being a catalytic leader.

TEAM

Many years ago, I heard the acronym TEAM explained this way: Together, Everyone Accomplishes More.

A unified team is a force to be dealt with.

Peyton Manning, the legendary Super Bowl winning quarterback and five-time NFL Most Valuable Player, said, "Leaders, you must understand the sustained power and influence that comes from your relationships with other people." Your words have power. Your influence is greater than you might think. And as a leader, what you do affects more than just you. You are a critical driver of TEAM unity and focus.

One of my recent focuses with our team has been on building and maintaining a sustainable pace, organizationally and individually as leaders. I believe too often the church (as well as other companies and organizations) just keeps adding and adding to what we do, crowding the calendar and swamping people's lives. That is not how you honor and love one another. That's how you burn people out.

By focusing on building and maintaining a sustainable pace, it means we say no to a lot of things, many of them very good things! But if we attempted to do them, we would overtax our team members and our volunteers, and that's not the goal. We want our team members to have margin, not live in a constant state of being overwhelmed. We want their home lives and relationships to be healthy. We want their families to celebrate their part in accomplishing the mission of the church. I believe that's part of what it means to remain people and team focused as a leader.

Now this involves conversation—honest, transparent conversation about margin, workload, and life. Be careful that you do not overlay your assumptions on your team members. Don't say their no for them; you might be surprised by what they come back with when you make your ask.

Andy Stanley notes, "Every single leader has power. Your words as a leader can weigh 100 or 10,000 pounds. Every time you use your power, you're using it for somebody—either for yourself, or for others. Great leaders leverage their influence and power for the benefit of other people."[5]

When you consider and make decisions, and when you communicate, are you using your influence and power for the benefit of those on your team or for yourself? That answer matters.

Hiring

Hiring is one of the most impactful tasks a leader will do.

Horst Schultze, the cofounder of the Ritz-Carlton company, has said, "We don't hire people; we select people."[6] That's intentional choice. It's not accidental or haphazard. It's purposeful.

In his classic book *Good to Great,* Jim Collins reminds us that hiring is critical. "First who; then what. Not first what, then who."[7] Particularly for mission-driven work, he notes that your work is too important to entrust to the wrong people. He's famous for his line that we have to "get the right people in the right seats on the bus," increasing our standards, not compromising them.

For several decades now, I've operated with a framework when it comes to hiring new team members. It's called the 5 Cs.[8]

1. Calling

This is specific to the church context where I lead. Is this person called by God to this role? If not, they're going to bail when the going gets tough. (Spoiler: there are tough days for every leader, even in church world.) Are they confident in their calling for this season to lead in this role? It doesn't have to be forever, either in a specific role or in a specific location. But they do have to have a sense of calling.

If you're not leading in a local church context, for your team, this might be a strong sense of commitment to your organization's mission or purpose. This might be a strong sense of passion around the cause you exist to serve. Is this just going to be a job to them, or is it more? Is this position hitting the sweet spot of their gifts, passions, skills, and talents? Or are they just going to be treading water in this role?

It is a leader's job to stay inspired and to stay crystal clear about our calling and commitment as a leader. When we are clear on this, we can stand firm, immovable. But it is a leader's responsibility to be clear about this for themselves. No one else can do it for you. No one else can clarify or strengthen your calling but you.

Remember, a motivated employee outworks an unmotivated employee by an average of 43 percent.[9] A committed leader who is clear about their calling, passion, and motivation is what you want. It's contagious for your other team members and those you serve. Don't settle for less.

2. Character

This is a *big* deal; much bigger than I hear too many leaders giving it credit for. If a leader's gifts or skills outpace their character development, that is a train wreck waiting to happen. Have you ever seen a gifted leader who had a moral failing, an ethical lapse, or a defect that "suddenly" affected their job? It's never sudden, though it does seem that way. It's the result of consistent pressures coming from a lack of alignment between beliefs, words, and actions.

Character is a nonnegotiable for any leader I'm going to hire. I believe strongly in second chances, but leadership positions are not ideal ground for character reclamation projects. Too much is at risk, and the ripples can affect so many other people, in addition to the mission itself.

Craig Groeschel said, "Talent can get you to the top, but only character can keep you there."[10] I believe that character is often overlooked in favor of tremendous skill and competency.

But the bill always comes due. A strong moral compass will be evident over time, and the presence (or absence) of one will communicate loud and clear to the team.

Character failures often make headlines in church world. But they also make headlines in the political sphere, in the corporate world, in entertainment, and in the nonprofit sector. Why? We know that character matters. And when a leader makes a misstep here, it affects so much more than just them. Carey Nieuwhof notes, "No one will ever pay you to work on your character. But they will fire you if you don't."[11]

Catalytic leaders work far more on their character than on their competency. Nieuwhof again: "Character, not competency, determines capacity."[12]

3. Competency

While this might be the first one on your list, it's not on mine. It matters, to be sure. We want people to be able to do the job we're hiring them to do. If someone's going to lead our worship band, I want them to be able to sing. And it's a nonnegotiable—competency matters. I believe that excellence honors God and inspires people, and though I don't demand or expect perfection, competency in their role is the floor of my expectations. But I expect team members to grow intentionally, and never be satisfied with their current level of competence.

A leader cannot exist by passion alone, but they cannot exist without passion. And competency is often where passion is on display.

This might be the easiest of the Cs to measure. But then again, I've discovered that some candidates interview really well. Reference checks will unearth good information here, especially if you go deeper than the list the candidate provides.

I will often ask a reference, "Can you think of anyone else I can talk with who could speak to this candidate's character/competency?" I'm usually pleasantly surprised at how willing people are to share information. And too often, we don't have the information simply because we didn't ask. To get the right answers, we have to ask the right questions.

Is this leader leveraging their gifts, passion, skills, and talents for something bigger than themselves and their own benefit/career/future? That's a key question at the heart of the competence element for me as I assess.

4. Chemistry

We put candidates into environments, both structured and unstructured, with other team members, and then we ask those team members for feedback. Did you enjoy spending time with them? Do you think you would enjoy working together? We put candidates through several personality and work assessments (the DISC and Working Genius), and we put great stock in the feedback we get around chemistry. More than once, we've waved off a candidate that was strong in every other C because we didn't see a strong chemistry with the rest of the team.

We'll take a candidate out to lunch or dinner, and we'll include all of our spouses whenever possible. I've found that this is a great way to exponentially increase your chances of spotting a great potential hire, or to spot red flags that you might miss in interviews or on Zoom calls. More eyes and ears from a diverse group will see and hear far more than any one individual.

This is also where we're going to look at emotional intelligence (EQ), what Daniel Goleman describes as "how you manage yourself and how you manage your relationships."[13] A candidate's EQ will help us assess what kind of leader a candidate is, how they will work with peers on the team, and what they will replicate as they recruit and develop new leaders. Emotions are contagious, and because of that, we are going to look for emotional self-awareness in a potential leader on our team.

5. Culture

This is the newest of the 5 Cs. I haven't always included this one, but experience taught me the value of it.

Every organization, every business, every church, and every team has a unique culture. We might talk a good game about our vision, values, and strategy, but Peter Drucker was right: "Culture eats strategy for breakfast."[14]

Learning what your culture is matters a great deal more than most leaders think, and adding new people will highlight areas of culture that you might not have been aware of. We want new team members to fit the culture we have intentionally designed and created, so we have extensive conversations around this.

For example, here are some elements of our team's culture:

- We work hard. And we have fun.
- We believe the mission matters, that excellence honors God and inspires people, and we give our work our best.
- We give "the last 10%" of honesty with one another. The first 90% is usually easy; it's the last 10% when we hesitate to really share, but that last 10% is where the magic is.
- We believe in and are *for* one another.

If you don't believe a culture fit matters, then just hire a few people who are not culture fits. You'll see soon enough!

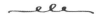

It takes a lot longer to vet candidates through this 5 C framework. But I've found that it is worth it. And in the past when I compromised one or more of the Cs, usually because "we just really need someone right now," it's always a mistake and ends up being a short-term hire, which means we have to do this all over again. It's always better to do it right the first time than cycle through people, which has a tremendously negative effect on organizational mission and momentum (not to mention the exorbitant financial and emotional cost of a misfit hire).

The US Department of Labor estimates the cost of a wrong hire at 30 percent of that team member's first year salary.[15] Thirty percent! Jorgen Sundberg, of LINK humans, went even further; he said that the cost of recruiting, hiring, and onboarding a new employee can be as much as $240,000![16] So, reality is somewhere in that ballpark range. In either case, I'm not interested in wasting resources like that. So, our hiring process takes longer and is more thorough. We've had candidates drop out partway through many times. But I believe we're getting better at finding the right fit based on our 5 C evaluation framework.

Remember too, what you win them with, you win them to. You are setting expectations during the hiring process of what working with you and your team is going to be like. Be mindful of that as you have meetings and conversations. Don't be the leader who paints a rosy picture and then, once the first week is over, exhibits a reality that is far different from what was advertised. Be realistic, honest, and authentic as you hire. You'll never regret that.

The Ideal Team Player

I also like Patrick Lencioni's framework for *The Ideal Team Player* (found in his book by that name, which I *highly* recommend). In short, you're looking for the intersection of three traits: humble, hungry, and smart.

• Humble: Lacking excessive ego or concern about status. Recognizing what is true. Not thinking less of yourself but thinking of yourself less.

• Hungry: Strong work ethic; hates being thought of as a slacker. Always thinking of the next step and the next opportunity.

• Smart: This is emotional intelligence (EQ), not IQ. It's people smarts.

These are team skills, and as I've learned more about how to identify and encourage these traits in our team members, I've valued them more and more. None are negotiable; all are critical for a great team player and leader.

When You're New

From Tim Elmore at GrowingLeaders.com: "According to the US Department of Labor, during the months of April, May, and June of 2021, a total of 11.5 million workers quit their jobs. Recent studies indicate it's likely not over. A survey of over 30,000 workers conducted by Microsoft found that 54 percent are considering quitting; Gallup found that 48 percent of employees are actively searching for new opportunities. Persio reported that 38 percent of participants plan to make a change in the next six months."[17]

That is a significant number of employees who are saying that they'd rather be somewhere else.

What does The Great Resignation mean for leaders? What should we be thinking about with regard to our teams, our organizational health, and our own personal leadership?

One question I've gotten from leaders who are considering a move, or who have just made a move, is, "What are some things I can do to make this a solid, positive start as I begin with a new team or organization?"

I believe asking the right questions is how you get the right answers. And this is the right question.

It doesn't matter if you are a new leader or a leader with decades of experience; this list is helpful for any leader making a move.

1. Connect with People

John Maxwell describes this as putting people first. It's easy to get bogged down in tasks, goals, planning—but people are the main thing for any organization.

As you begin as a new leader for a team or organization, prioritize connecting with people. Listen to their stories, their dreams, and their hearts. As you get to know them, you will learn how best to lead them to accomplish the necessary tasks and goals.

Assume the best about people. I know, I know, you should never assume. Except in this case. Start with this mindset: I will assume the best about this person. It will make a big difference in how you can connect with them.

2. Be Clear

Dave Ramsey said, "Clarity is kindness."[18] We often try to be nice and soft-pedal at first. Resist that urge. Be clear. Be clear about expectations, as you review performance, as you set goals, as you share feedback. Not knowing where you stand is incredibly frustrating. Not knowing what the goals are or how you're doing with regard to achieving them is even more so.

3. Evaluate Ruthlessly but Quietly

This does *not* mean that you share all your evaluative thoughts at first. Remember Stephen Covey's timeless advice: "Seek first to understand, then to be understood."[19] You might not know the whole story or why things are done a certain way. Listen. Make notes, evaluate, mind-map ideas, for sure. But keep your own counsel at first. Write things down in a journal or notepad for your eyes only for now.

Coming into a new team or organization, you're going to have what I call "fresh eyes." Those are invaluable. Often over time we don't see what is blindingly obvious to someone new. Write down what you observe. Take notes after conversations or at the end of the day when thoughts are freshest. What needs to be updated? What needs to go? What needs to be added? What needs to change?

Evaluate ruthlessly—but quietly at first.

4. Ask Good Questions

A new leader needs to be *full* of questions! "Why" should be one of the most used words in your vocabulary. Take notes as you ask and listen. In my experience, the best leaders always have something to write with and write on. Fill that notebook, that Evernote note, or that binder up. There's a lot you don't know yet. And the people around you have deep institutional knowledge of why things are done this way here, why this matters there, and why we never talk about that elephant in the corner over there. Ask questions and listen to their stories. You'll gain tremendous insight and wisdom.

Leaders are insatiable learners. Asking good questions is a phenomenal and effective way to learn.

Is the Grass Really Greener?

Every time I talk to leaders, I am reminded of what a privilege and a challenge leadership really is. It's humbling and exciting to lead others in an organization to accomplish a mission. Anyone can be critical and spot problems, but a leader gets on the solution side and finds a way to address them, seeing them as opportunities for what could be.

Elmer Towns said, "Don't leave something; go *to* something."[20]

It's not hard to find things we don't like about an environment, a place, or a job. I had a high school teacher who told us, "There will always be things about every job you don't like. But if there's more than 10 percent of the job that is like that, find a new one." For him, it was wearing a tie. He was required to, so he did. But he hated it. But if that's the worst thing about the job, is it worth leaving? Not for him. And he poured into me and so many other students, to our lasting benefit.

I see a tendency among many people to see that the grass is greener elsewhere. I get that—I think it's a temptation common to all humankind. Especially in a season when things are challenging on multiple fronts, the grass can seem so much better over there. A fresh start, a new beginning, a clean slate.

But is it true?

Towns' advice is worth remembering. "Don't leave something; go *to* something." If you run from challenges, you'll never stop. If you run from discomfort, you'll never stop.

If you're running *to* something, that's great! That's exciting. The passion around a new adventure, the sense that this next chapter could be the best yet—that's what you want. But if you're just running *from* something, be very careful because you could find yourself bouncing from job to job every three to four years, trying to find what you'll only find if you stay in one place long enough.

It's rarely the leaders who bounce from place to place every three years who make the biggest impact.

I've discovered that the greatest growth in a leader is often when they are tenacious, when they persist through difficulty, and they refuse to let challenges derail them.

Is leadership tough? Absolutely. That's why most people don't do it.

As I have mentioned throughout this book, I strongly believe that every leader needs a coach. I've had a leadership coach for years, and the benefits I have seen from this are truly immeasurable, especially during a season like we've experienced through the COVID pandemic, social unrest, lockdowns, quarantines, and cultural divisiveness. This has been one of the most difficult seasons of my career, and I know many of you would agree that it's been a difficult season for you as well.

My coach has helped me to have perspective during difficult days, to remember my why, and to stay focused on the "blocking and tackling" that are critical. It's really hard to see the whole picture when you're in the frame; that's the value of an outside perspective, and a leadership coach has brought that value to me.

Persistence makes a difference. Don't make excuses; step it up. I love how Horst Schultze puts it: "We are leaders. We have forfeited the right to make excuses."[21]

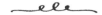

Chapter Nine

Never Stop Leading Change

I t's been said that no one likes change, unless it's their idea!
Thomas Edgley wrote, "Change or die." Such a short quote—
but direct and to the point, isn't it?

Yet people resist change.

I laughingly say that my sense of style got stuck at one point in
my life and hasn't moved since. If my wife wasn't so
intentional about making sure that I had clothes that were made
in this century, I imagine I would be wearing the same clothes
I wore twenty years ago. It's not that I don't like to look nice; I
just don't want to change what I'm used to wearing. My
favorite shoes are my tennis shoes, and I don't know if that
will ever change. I'm not immune to change resistance, and I
bet you're not either.

The fact is change is a part of life. I dare say very few of us are
using the same cell phone we had ten years ago. We typically
will replace them every two to four years. I had a bag phone, I
had a flip phone, I had a blackberry, I had an Android, and now
I have an iPhone. As phones have changed, so have we. And

phones are not the only things that change in our world. In fact, it might be easier to list the things that don't change.

Humans like stability. We like the stability of regular nutrition, living indoors, and a steady paycheck. When any of those are threatened, we respond, usually in an emotion-driven way. And yet, when we *choose* to change what we eat, where we live, or where we work, we can be excited about it. In those cases, change is our idea.

I have lived in four different states and quite a few different cities. Since we've lived in Virginia, we've rented five different apartments or townhouses before we bought the house we live in now. That's a lot of change of address forms in seventeen years! But each time, we chose that change, especially when we decided to plant some roots and buy a house. That was our idea, not someone else's.

Here's what you as a leader need to know. Change is inevitable in your team and your organization. You can either acknowledge that and lead it, or you can try to resist it and eventually get pulled along anyway. That's why the ninth key to catalytic leadership is to **never stop leading change**.

Carey Nieuwhof said, "Organizations that don't change become museums to another era."[1]

The first time I ever visited England, we visited Westminster Abbey and Big Ben, we saw the Tower Bridge and London Bridge, and we were reminded to "mind the gap" as we rode the Tube. One of the things that surprised me as we visited a number of old churches was that many of them were only tourist attractions; there was no active church there. And for the ones that did still host an active church, the gatherings were very small: single or lower double-digit attendance. Of course, that's not every church in England; some are thriving! But for a country that had such an outsized impact on Christian thought and influence, that really surprised me. But not as much as this: England today is said to be four percent Christian. Four percent!

What happened?

There are lots of answers to that question; it's not a simple one. But at the root, I believe the reason the church did not grow, thrive, and expand in our era there is this: they rejected change. Jack Welch said, "When the rate of change on the outside [of an organization] exceeds the rate of change on the inside, the end is near."[2] At minimum, irrelevance is the result. And that's what I believe happened. The church became irrelevant over time to the people around them, and they stopped influencing because they stopped changing. (This does not advocate for changing theology or doctrine in the case of a church, by the way. I'm talking about the model of ministry, not the core beliefs).

Growth means change. And yet, as John Maxwell has famously said, "Everybody wants to grow, but nobody wants to change."[3]

I've watched churches wrestle with and reject change much of my life. I've seen what happens when change is poorly communicated and executed. And I've seen what happens when change is rejected and disregarded. In both cases, the organization suffers and many times dies. Leading change in an organization is not for the faint of heart, especially change in a church setting.

Leadership is a skill, and like any skill, it can and should be developed. But that takes intentional growth. It takes intentional decisions to pursue growth through what we read, who we spend time with, and what we spend time doing.

Jim Collins notes, "Building something great is not a function of your circumstances. It is a function of your choices and your discipline."[4] Don't miss that: your choices *and* your discipline. That's your willingness to do what you know needs to be done, regardless of how you might feel at a given moment.

What needs to change? How do you know what to tackle first, second, third, and so on?

Max DePree said that one of the first jobs of a leader is to "define reality as it is, not as you wish it were."[5] To know what needs to change, we first have to determine what's working and what's not, what's bearing fruit and what's not, what's producing the results we seek and what's not. Peter Drucker said, "The most important leadership decisions are not made; they are apparent."[6] Leaders know.

Try this exercise. Take out a blank sheet of paper. Spend ten minutes—no more—and list everything you would change right now about your company, team, church, or organization if the sky was the limit and there were no barriers. If you could change *anything*, what would be the first things you would change?

How many did you list?

Most leaders have no problem listing at least ten things right off the bat. Some more, some less, but typically at least ten.

Now, what can you do about one or two of those today or this week?

Bill Gates said, "Most people overestimate what they can do in one year and underestimate what they can do in ten years." Great leaders don't whimper and complain. They take the steps they need to take to make the changes they know need to be made. Craig Groeschel notes, "If you want results that no one else is getting, you have to do things no one else is doing."[7]

Are most of your conversations with team members, with your staff, and with your board about survival, maintaining what is? Or are they about what could be but isn't yet, and how to get there?

Never stop leading change, leaders. It's worth it on the other side.

A(nother) Bylaws Revision

Governing documents for any organization are not exciting at all, but they are really important. There are certain changes that can come about only by starting the process at the level of those documents.

When I came to Southview, there was a team that had been working on a bylaws revision for three years. One of my assigned tasks was to help that team get to the finish line, which we did after eighteen months. After a long press and more meetings than I care to remember, that felt great, and I was content to never touch those documents again.

The problem is that leaders can never stop leading change. And this was no exception to that key principle.

Over the next dozen years, we began to see operational issues that we did not foresee during our revision process. We began to see governance challenges and unexpected problems that popped up. We had to consider, do we do this again? Do we go back and review, seeing where we needed to make adjustments based on now having some real-world track with the new model? After much discussion, that's what we decided to do. But it was not easy.

As with any organizational change, there were people who were all for it, and there were people who were strongly opposed.

Such is the life and work of a leader.

And such is the life and work of a leader who never stops leading change.

Over time, the changes were strategized, communicated, socialized, and ultimately passed. The church and our mission benefited, no doubt in my mind, but it came at a cost. Every change does.

That doesn't mean we don't make the necessary moves. It doesn't mean we don't lead necessary change. But it does mean we need to count the cost and realize that there always is a cost.

Vision

John Maxwell has said, "Leaders see more than others see, and they see before others see."[8] That's vision. It's a leader's job to cast vision, to paint a picture of the preferred future for the organization they lead, for the mission and purpose they want to see accomplished. Proverbs 29:18 (KJV) says, "where there is no vision, the people perish." So do businesses, organizations, and churches. I like Andy Stanley's definition of vision: "A mental picture of what *could be* fueled by the conviction it *should be*."[9]

What happens when a leader loses the vision? The organization they lead begins to drift. And no company, organization, church, or leader *ever* drifted into significance and impact. Martin Luther King Jr. said, "Change will never roll in on the wheels of inevitability."[10]

That's why a leader can never stop leading change. There's always the next hill to take, the next touchdown to score, the next mountain to climb! A leader does not settle for what is, maintaining the machine, waiting for someone else to make it happen; a leader is always seeing what could be and moving forward to see it become reality!

I've seen far too many leaders settle, believing the change will not happen or that it cannot be achieved. They settle in for a life that is less than what they were designed to do, and that is always a tragedy. They maintain *what is* rather than reach for and lead to what *could be and should be*.

Rorke Denver, a Navy SEAL commander and author, advises, "Limit your field of vision and you will see more."[11] I think part of the challenge for leaders is the depth and breadth of the myriad details they face on a daily basis. By determining to intentionally limit what you're looking at, what you are directly overseeing details of, you not only create new leadership opportunities for new and emerging leaders, you free up your mental margin to see more than others can and before others can. As Andy Stanley puts it, "Leaders do less to accomplish more."[12] Reduce your breadth of focus, and your depth will grow significantly.

When it comes to those you lead, you must never forget what Jeff Henderson wrote: "Vision leaks over time, as does inspiration. The natural drift of any organization is toward confusion and complexity."[13] Leaders keep the vision the main thing. They celebrate the wins, refocus when there's a lack of clarity or confusion, and keep things simple to ensure alignment and prevent mission drift.

Incremental Change

I've long admired the concept of *kaizen*.

Kaizen is a Japanese term meaning "change for the better" or "continuous improvement." I first heard it in connection with Toyota and how they strongly encourage every employee to submit suggestions for improving the car production process. From team members on the assembly line to those in the offices, if someone sees something, no matter how small, that could add to their operational efficiency, they will value and consider it. They believe *kaizen,* or continuous improvement, is something that every team member has a hand in, and they believe that this gradual, methodical process of getting better is the way to go.

Jonathan Milligan writes, "Consistency is the mother of momentum."[14] Every leader wants to experience organizational momentum. And *kaizen* is a model for consistent, continual improvement over time.

I applied that principle to my own leadership. I believed that slow, methodical, consistent change and improvement over time would yield great results. And I did see some of that. But here's where I would go back in time and give myself a piece of advice if I could.

Taking change slowly does *not* always mean people will accept it more easily or that they will remain a part of your team or organization.

As every parent knows and has probably told their child, sometimes the best thing to do is rip the Band-Aid off, even if it hurts more for a moment.

I can think of many, many times when I did not take a step that I knew needed to be taken because I wanted to take the change process slowly. I chose to navigate change gently with people, believing that if I led the change slowly enough, they would accept it and stick with me and the organization through it.

Do you know what I learned?

Most of the time, people who disagree with the change will leave anyway.

By prolonging the change process, I prolonged the pain of the change process. And people are not fans of prolonged pain.

As Kirbyjon Caldwell said, "If there's anything worse than a bad decision, it is a bad decision made slowly!"

These days, when I think through change timelines, I think (with the benefit of hindsight and experience), that if you want to see significant results, it requires significant change. And timing matters. To prolong the pain of change is often *not* the right decision.

Carey Nieuwhof asks two poignant questions with regard to change and leading through it: "Is it more frightening to lose a handful of people, or to never accomplish your mission? Will you allow ten people to destroy the future of 10,000 who remain unreached?"[15]

Nobel Laureate Malala Yousafzai has been a longtime proponent for the rights of girls to receive an education. Her determination, even the face of opposition by the Taliban in her home country, has led to her prominence on the international stage, where she is known for her courage in refusing to be silenced. She speaks clearly and forcefully for needed change on this critical issue. I once heard her say, "If you want change, what are you waiting for?"[16] There is so much wisdom there.

Leaders, if you know there is necessary change that will help your organization make a difference, if you know that a particular change will improve organizational effectiveness, then what indeed are you waiting for?

Don't let the people who left and abandoned you decide who you will become or how you lead. If you're leading from a place of pain or discouragement because of people who aren't even there anymore, it's time to find a counselor to help you process that so you can move forward. The people you lead deserve your best, and if you're trapped in the pain of the past, you're not giving it to them.

It takes discernment and wisdom to know when it's time to move out on change and I find great wisdom in the counsel of other wise leaders. I believe this is a strength of the team leadership model: where the organization is not limited by the gifts of a single leader but benefit from the breadth of gifts that a team of leaders possesses. I have consistently been blessed and encouraged by other leaders around our table who use their gifts for the benefit of the whole team. When we make a decision, I have so much more confidence in it, knowing that we've all weighed in and this is the best decision we can make, given what we know right now. It is a rare decision that is made with 100% certainty. If you're waiting for that before you move, you will likely never move. But the advantage of the wisdom of a team who is on board with the vision and mission and weighs in is incalculable to me.

Honest and ruthless evaluation of the current results will indicate where change is needed. I referenced W. Edward Deming's quote earlier: "Your system is perfectly designed to give you the results you are currently getting." If you don't like the results, it's time to change the system(s) that yielded them. Rorke Denver also speaks to this. He notes that leaders have to "make bold corrections to get bold results."[17] I think too often in the past, I've resisted bold decisions and corrections in an effort to keep the peace a little longer. I've committed to learn from that, knowing that making the right decision for the team and the organization matters so much more than temporary "peace."

The Lazy River of Mediocrity

If you think things are good, that you can just coast for a season, then you are likely in the lazy river of mediocrity.

I like the lazy river rides at water parks. Have you ever been on one of those? You just sit in an inner tube and float, gently, calmly, serenely, going through the water slowly, just following the drift of the easy current. It's so peaceful. And given that so much of my mental life is characterized by movement, often at a high velocity, the lazy river is a wonderful diversion.

But that is not where catalytic leaders are intended to live.

Can you imagine never moving any faster than the water in the lazy river moves? That's what satisfaction with mediocrity looks like. And that's what it looks like when a leader stops leading change.

The lazy river is a wonderful break and diversion from the fast-paced life of a leader. Just don't aspire to stay long term and live there. There's nothing catalytic to be found in the lazy river.

Change Is an Opportunity

The COVID pandemic was the most significant period of organizational change I have seen in my lifetime. For leaders, I believe they were some of the toughest we might experience. And the logical question after an experience like that is, "Now what? What's the way forward from here?"

Over the last year, I've heard a lot of leaders, and not a few pastors, express their desire to return to life as it was before COVID. "If only we could get back to what things were like in February of 2020!" "When will things get back to normal?" "I'm so ready to get back in person and get things back like they were before."

During the pandemic, I came across a quote from Amy Edmondson, the Novartis Professor of Leadership at Harvard University's Business School. It captured some of what I've been feeling and what we've been discussing around our leadership table. She wrote, "Too many are asking whether we will go back to normal. To me, the problematic word is 'back.' There is no going back to pre-COVID times. There is only forward—to a new and uncertain future that is currently presenting us with an opportunity for thoughtful design."[18]

That last part is what we've been discussing for nearly a year at Southview. This has been a season of tremendous loss and difficulty for so many. And the church has engaged like I've rarely seen. I've watched as food pantries have been filled, children have been cared for, the poor have been served, and teachers, nurses, and first responders have been honored and blessed in tangible ways. I've watched as hospitals have been provided with supplies they need, as homeless shelters have been stocked with needed items, and as school supplies have been collected and distributed. We have not allowed what we cannot do to stop us from doing what we can. And in that, I find great connection with Edmondson's words. "An opportunity for thoughtful design." I love that phrase, and I'm resonating with it at a deep level. After a difficult, trying season, those words are echoing in my spirit.

I've been asking our leaders for months, "What does the church you want to attend look like? What would it feel like, sound like, smell like? If today you were choosing a church to invest in, describe it. And let's build that." I'm inviting our teams to re-dream the dream. We have an opportunity for a fresh start as we "reboot" our physical campus. What needs to stay the same? What needs to change? What do we need to keep doing? What do we need to stop doing?

I've always been drawn to the Old Testament prophets, and I find encouragement and hope so often in their words. Isaiah 43:18–19 has been on my mind and lips a lot this year. "Forget the former things; do not dwell on the past. See, I am doing a new thing! Now it springs up; do you not perceive it? I am making a way in the wilderness and streams in the wasteland."

It's been a tough season. No doubt. But God's not done. He's making a way forward. We have an opportunity to lead in fresh ways. The only thing stopping us is us.

We have tremendous freedom in this season to try new things, to explore new ideas, to attempt what we never have before. We will fail at times. But we might also find that God takes our efforts and does something with them that is unmistakably Him. Something remarkable.

As we enter a new chapter, post-pandemic, I want to challenge you, leaders: don't miss the wonder and invitation of Edmondson's quote. We have, right now, "an opportunity for thoughtful design." How will you thoughtfully design your leadership going forward? It doesn't have to look like it always has. The world has changed. We have changed, you and I. And we can step forward differently, with great intention and purpose. Never stop leading change.

Chapter Ten

Prioritize Clear Communication

For leaders, communication is critical. It's an everyday part of life. We communicate in writing, in person, by phone, email, and text. We communicate with small groups and large, in one-on-one meetings and with other leaders.

Communication involves sharing information. But it's more than just the dissemination of information—it involves communicating for the purpose of inspiring change. (See Andy Stanley's excellent book on this topic, *Communicating for a Change*). The tenth key to catalytic leadership is to **prioritize clear communication**.

In 2014, I went on a sabbatical. This is an intentional, planned season for pastors and academics to pull aside from the normal grind of everyday life and focus on a project, on intentional rest, or on new connections. During my sabbatical, I finished a book manuscript that I had been working on, I went on a month-long archaeological dig in Jordan, I stopped by London on the way home to do some research for my dissertation, and I spent some intentional time with my wife and daughters. It was a life-giving season for me, and truly helped me prepare for what was (unknowingly at the time) going to be the most difficult next seven years in my ministry journey.

Before I left, our team had a solid plan for taking care of my normal responsibilities. From preaching to staff leadership, from board meetings to the rest, we thought we had all the bases covered. But sometimes, you don't know what you don't know—until you learn.

One of my roles is to keep an eye on our overall financial health. I don't get down in the weeds with it, but I look at a high level how things stand financially each month. I can spot if something is a red flag with overspending, or I note and address when income begins to slip. Everyone knew this, and everyone agreed to keep an eye on it. But the problem is that when it's everyone's responsibility, it's ultimately no one's responsibility. So, it got missed for three months. I should say, I missed it, and in the process learned something really important.

When I came back from sabbatical, we discovered that giving (income) had slipped significantly, and expenses had been higher than normal, creating a gap of over $40,000. And over the next few months, because habits are not changed in a day, that would grow further to over $60,000. That was not a great season. We had just paid off the mortgage the previous year but did not yet have our cash reserves built up to the level we needed. That was a goal in process, and what we had saved got obliterated by this gap.

What do we do? We had meetings about next steps, brainstormed ideas, and came up with a lot of ways to address this. In the end, we determined that we would provide crystal-clear communication, as wide and broad as possible. We communicated through our small groups, through our email list, through social media, through our weekly gatherings, and through mail. We boiled it down to three options we saw going forward:

- **Sell the building and go portable.** This provides cash infusion and a "fresh start." The cost of maintaining the building and grounds is not small; this would reduce expenses and provide a significant income (one time). The negatives are significant; having a home base for ministry operations is useful, and changing to a portable church model was something none of us had any experience doing.

- **Lay off staff.** I liked this one the least because we had a strong and unified team that was committed to moving the ball up the field. We were on the same page, and we were all focused on seeing Southview become the church that we believe God intended for us to become. Getting rid of one or more key staff is a body blow to organizational momentum, so this was not my favorite.

- **Change the story.** If you don't like the story you're currently writing, you can change it by changing what you're doing. By increasing the habit of generosity for more of the people who called Southview home, we believed we could turn this around. We wrote a sermon series of teachings around the theme of story changers and how Jesus changed our story and intends for us to be story changers in our world. We wrote small group curriculum to align all of our groups to focus on story changing. We kept it in front of people in as many ways as we could, as often as we could.

We laid all three options out, as clearly as possible. The choice would be up to us, and we'd all see what the choice was by what happened next.

What did we see? We saw people respond to that clarity and transparency. We didn't close the gap completely by year's end, but we came close, and the next six months proved it was not a gimmick or "one-off." Prioritizing clear and transparent communication works.

Effective Communication

Several decades ago, I attended the "Communicating in Today's Reality" conference at Willow Creek Community Church. The conference was designed to help those who communicate regularly in churches, businesses, or other organizations to get better at communication. At the time, I was serving on staff at a church in Texas, and I wanted to get better at what I saw to be a critically important skill. That investment is one I've never regretted. Did it improve my communication? Well, I think so, but I know that depends on who you talk to. It really did clarify so many things in my mind around the topic of effective communication.

One of the speakers at that conference was Ken Davis. Here are three of the principles that really impacted me when I first heard Ken speak.

1. "If you're going to stand and deliver, you must deliver with crystal-clear focus."[1]

How many times have I messed this up! A seminary professor named Howard Hendricks used to say it this way: "a mist in the pulpit is a fog in the pew." If communicators and teachers are not communicating with crystal-clear focus (a mist), then by the time the hearers hear it, it's just a fog; it can't be grasped at all. Clarity is critically important. This doesn't just happen; it takes hard work to get to this level of simplicity and coherence.

One of my goals when I communicate is to take something complicated and make it simple, sticky, and portable. Simple enough so anyone can understand it; sticky so that it will be memorable beyond an hour from now; and portable, so you'll be able to take it with you and have it accessible when you need it. That takes a lot of time. In fact, I would estimate that it takes 25 percent of my total prep time to boil down what I've learned and want to communicate into a format that is simple, sticky, and portable.

Ken noted, "A survey was done of 2,500 people coming out of church: 75% of people couldn't say what the point was in a sentence. 50% of pastors couldn't say what the point was in a sentence. If you can't say in one sentence what the point is, you can't do it in thirty minutes."[2]

Crafting one-point statements that are memorable and sticky is challenging. But if we don't spend the time and do it, we'll find that the main idea that we struggled with will float out of people's minds very quickly. Sometimes, before they leave the room.

This can be incredibly discouraging for communicators. To know that what we communicate won't stick long is tough to hear. But if we spend the time to make our one-point clear, and to make it sticky and memorable, we'll find that it will remain with our listeners far longer.

2. "Ask others to critique you."[3]

Every week at Southview, our staff fills out an evaluation form where we think through how every element of the weekend went. From our First Impressions team to our kids ministry, from our student ministry to our weekend services, we evaluate *everything*. And that includes the sermon. Nothing is out of bounds or off limits.

I've found it incredibly helpful to get feedback on what worked in the sermon, what didn't, what was helpful, and what could have been left out. It's not always what I'd like to hear, but it's almost always what I need to hear. While this is subjective, it's very helpful to get different perspectives. But if

I didn't ask for the critique, I likely wouldn't get it, especially when it's constructive. We have to ask. And then we have to listen in a teachable posture.

3. "Who killed the Bible people? We did! We suck all of the emotion and drama out of the people and stories."[4]

This idea changed the way I read the Bible. When I read, I try hard to read it with emotion, with passion, with feeling; like I would if I were telling a story that happened to me the other day. I believe the accounts in the Bible really happened, just like a story I might share of something that happened when I was at the grocery store, and I need to communicate it with the same level of passion and feeling. When we read it in a tired, monotone way, or we create a big difference in how we read the text and how we tell a story, we communicate that there's a big difference between what happens to me and what happened to people then.

Leaders know how important communication is. And the best way I know to get better at communication and leadership is to get around people who are further down the road than you are so you can learn from them. That's why I go to conferences like the Global Leadership Summit and Leadercast, and that's why I read books about leadership and communication. Leaders, getting better doesn't just happen; it's up to you to invest in yourself and your leadership.

Intentionally Growing as a Communicator

Occasionally, I'll get a question from young or new leaders about how to grow as a communicator. What's the best way to do that?

The advice I give is pretty consistent and has been for a long time.

First, listen to and watch as many great communicators as you can. As I was learning to speak publicly, I voraciously devoured as many sermons, speeches, and talks as I could get my hands on. Today, with thousands of podcasts, TED Talks, and YouTube videos at our fingertips, there's no excuse for someone who wants to learn to speak with more authority, confidence, and power. Listen to as many great communicators as you can. Try out what you hear; begin to experiment with different facets of communication style. As you do, you'll discover what fits you and what doesn't.

Over time, you'll learn to recognize the organizing patterns of speeches, talks, and sermons. You'll learn which oratorical and rhetorical flourishes connect with you, and which ones don't. You'll discover which ones feel natural for you and which ones make you feel like you're wearing someone else's clothes. This is all part of the learning. As you observe, make notes on what you like, what you don't like, and what you'd like to try yourself.

(And this advice is not just for those learning to speak. I still do this because I want to continue to get better).

Second, find some trusted people to give you feedback. Remember, ruthless evaluation is how we get better at leadership and at communication. Evaluate content, stories and illustrations, delivery, facial expressions, eye contact, hand gestures, body language, everything. If you need to hire a coach to help you in this area, it's worth the investment. Those who listen to you regularly will be grateful for your intentional investment in growing as a communicator.

My wife Charlotte has been a tremendous help to me in this area for decades. I know she will give me the honest, unvarnished truth in love when she hears me speak. Her feedback and suggestions have helped me far more than I could ever express, and anyone who hears me speak should realize how grateful they should be to her!

The staff team I work with at Southview is also really good about helping me to get better by giving me feedback. I regularly send out the text of my talk for their suggestions and feedback, and invariably their comments and insights make what I will communicate better.

Third, don't try to *be* your favorite communicator. It's one thing to learn from someone else; it's another to imitate them. Remember, God already created one of them—He didn't create two! You are created on purpose and designed to be *you*, and to communicate from *your* passions, skills, and gifts. Learn all you can from others, and over time, choose to intentionally develop your own communicative style.

It's inevitable that you will begin to use phrases that your favorite communicators use, and even patterns of speaking. Be aware of this, and over time, you will drop those "mimicking habits" in favor of your own style.

Fourth, practice every chance you get. I cannot tell you how many sermons I delivered to an empty room as I was learning to speak and preach. Over and over, week after week, month after month. It wasn't always fun, and I didn't always "feel like it," but over time, by doing the reps, I learned what worked and what didn't. I learned what felt comfortable for me and what didn't. I started speaking in small group settings, and then larger groups. Scripture teaches us not to "despise the day of small beginnings" (Zechariah 4:10). Public speaking is a skill that anyone can develop, but it must be developed! Even natural speakers can and should develop their skills to get even better.

Fifth, learn to read the room. As you speak, don't read your notes. Don't be so buried in your notes or screen that you're not paying attention to the body language of your audience. Whenever I speak, I make sure to have rehearsed what I'm going to say multiple times. That way, I can focus on reading the people in the room as I speak. I can pay attention to what idea or sentence or phrase connected, and which ones did not at all. I can look for people leaning forward, or for those leaning back with their eyes drooping. I can look for people who have what the longtime conductor of the Boston Philharmonic Orchestra, Benjamin Zander, calls "shining eyes," when they get what I'm saying and connect with it. As I speak, I can adjust what I'm saying to spend more time clarifying a point that hasn't landed yet for the majority of the room. I can drill a little deeper on something that created questioning or confused looks. I can build to a crescendo on something that connected really well. All of that is built on my reading the room as I speak, with every sentence.

This doesn't apply only in large public speaking venues; this also applies in meetings, on Zoom, and in one-on-one settings as well. Learning to read your audience will help you to lead better, to listen more effectively, and to speak more powerfully.

Sixth, review the video (or at least the audio) of your speech/talk/sermon if at all possible. This might mean setting up your phone to make a video from the back of the room. If all you can get is audio to review, that's better than nothing. If you're speaking at a venue where they record you, even better. Always get a copy if you can, and go back and watch it. You will discover a wealth of information that will help you get better.

Sometimes it's hand gestures that you are not even aware of making. Sometimes it's a speech pattern that you don't know you have. It could be that you're mumbling, that you're talking too fast or too slowly, too loudly or too softly. You might get this in feedback from others, but you might not. You will notice more by watching yourself than you might think.

You might be thinking, "I don't like to watch myself on video or listen to myself." Join the club! I don't either. I don't know anyone who really does. But if you want to get better, review is part of it. Remember, evaluated experience is what makes you better, not just repetition.

This is also where feedback is really helpful. While most people will tell you after you speak, "great job," or something equally kind, that's not going to help you get better. I always seek out specific feedback from people I trust. What landed well? What didn't? What could have been dropped? What needed more explanation?

I remember teaching my first Wednesday night Bible study in the first church I served. It was a small group of about a dozen people, and after I finished, I stepped out into the foyer area to chat with people as they left. I'll never forget what one older man said to me that day. As he was making his way out, I asked him if what I said made sense, looking for some feedback. He stopped, looked at me for a minute, and said, "Yeah, but you walk around too damn much." I have laughed about that for years. Honest, ruthless feedback indeed! But I've never forgotten it.

Clear communication is not a given; it comes from a leader who has worked on his or her craft and who has put the time in to "make it better."

Brief Is Better

There's an email shorthand that you might have seen (hopefully not in response to an email you sent). It's the acronym TL;DR, also seen sometimes as just TLDR. It stands for "too long; didn't read."

Ouch!

I've never gotten that as a reply, but I have gotten that feedback more than once over the years to an email (read: a tome) that I sent out. The feedback was kinder and gentler but conveyed that idea clearly. "Wow, that was really long. I tried to read it all, but I'm not sure I got everything because I fell asleep . . ."

From this, a lesson in prioritizing clear communication: brief is better.

There are a number of ways to make something in writing clear and brief. Perhaps it's using a numbered or bulleted list, or using bold or highlighted text to spotlight the main points or ideas; however you choose, you can make your written communication better and easier to scan and digest. It takes longer and requires some time for editing after you write. But isn't clear communication worth the extra time to get it right?

With regard to speaking, I will call out the elephant in the room up front: leaders like to talk! We love to communicate ideas, passion, vision, and strategy. We want to get as many people as we can as fired up as we can, and communication is one of the greatest tools to accomplish alignment.

That said, you can have too much of a good thing.

I don't know what the in-person equivalent of TL;DR is, but I've certainly experienced it when I sat through someone with a microphone going *far* beyond their allotted time and using way too many words to communicate their message with a lack of clarity. I've seen it in the faces and eyes of a group when

I've gone way too long. I needed to land the plane, not keep circling around the tower.

An experienced communicator friend once shared a piece of advice with me, and I've never forgotten it: "No one ever complains that a talk was too short. Get up, say what you need to say, say it well, and sit down."

Winston Churchill said, "If you want me to speak for two minutes, it will take me three weeks of preparation. If you want me to speak for thirty minutes, it will take me a week to prepare. If you want me to speak for an hour, I am ready now." What is behind that pearl of wisdom? Taking the needed time for preparation helps us distill our message and make it better.

Brief is better.

Fuzzy Communication

I've found that a lot of communication is fuzzy.

Sometimes it's between people who are married. Sometimes it's with colleagues. Sometimes it's between a team leader and the team.

What is fuzzy communication?

It's when the listener doesn't hear what the speaker is trying to say.

What's the reason for the fuzziness?

- It could be a lack of preparation on the communicator's part.
- It could be a lack of intentional listening on the listener's part.

- It could be environmental factors affecting where the communication is happening.

As noted above, remember: "Clarity is kindness."[5] To be clear is to be kind. I never want a team member to have to guess what I'm actually thinking or saying. I want them to know! And the best way for that to happen is for me to be clear.

Millions of freshmen learn in college speech classes that communication has three parts: what is said, what is heard, and what is meant. Far too often, those three are not the same. That's fuzzy communication. And Marcus Buckingham is spot on: "Clarity is the antidote to anxiety."[6] Too much anxiety on teams, in the workplace, and in marriages is because of fuzzy communication. That is both frustrating and fixable.

Clear communication is something that is chosen. It takes effort, preparation, and evaluation. It requires active listening on the part of those being communicated with, and it is always a work in progress. Communication can never be checked off as done "once and for all." Keep communicating with your team.

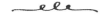

Chapter Eleven

Develop Other Leaders

The eleventh key to catalytic leadership is to **develop other leaders.**

I like how Craig Groeschel talked about this. He said, "If you don't want to develop leaders, then make all the decisions yourself. If you want your organization to reflect your weaknesses, then make all the decisions yourself."[1]

Every great leader I know invests themselves in developing other leaders.

Everything God puts in our lives is not just for us; it's for the benefit of those around us.

How can I take my experiences, my history, my track of decision making, my learnings, and help other leaders grow and thrive in their own leadership journey?

What happens if we *don't* develop other leaders? What happens if we just hang onto what we read, hear, learn, and experience for ourselves, and we never share it?

1. Other leaders don't get better.

Leadership is a team sport. While point leaders do carry a burden that is unique to their role, I have found that investing what I am learning in other leaders helps them grow as leaders, to get better in their own leadership, and to assist in carrying organizational leadership responsibilities.

2. We don't get better.

When I spend time investing in other leaders, every single time, I walk away learning something new or having something confirmed more strongly. Investing intentionally in developing other leaders helps me to become a better leader.

3. Our organization, company, church, or team doesn't benefit.

I have operated in a team leadership model for many years. There are some decisions that I have to make, to be sure, but I frequently seek the counsel and wisdom of other people on my team. That way, the decision is informed not by my gifts and experiences alone, but by all those around the table. I believe that benefits the organization I lead. While it doesn't ensure the right decision every time, it certainly increases the likelihood that we will make the best decision for the organization based on the information we have at the time.

When developing leaders bring me a challenge and want me to weigh in, my goal is always to ask first, "What do you think?" Developing critical and strategic thinking skills is so important for a leader, and the best way to learn is to do! I want to provide safe environments where leaders can make decisions that will not take down the ship but will help them build their leadership decision-making muscles so that they can eventually stand and then run on their own.

When one of my team or a leader I'm mentoring asks me to make a decision, more often than not, my response will be, "Your decision is the right one." Delegate as many decisions as you can, and push decisions as far down the organizational tree as you can. This communicates trust and value to your team members. Make as few decisions as you can, and hand off the rest.

If you have to be at the center of the spider web, where every thread touches or connects to you, that's not only unhealthy for you and your team, it's also completely unsustainable, and it does not scale for growth.

Potential

One of the most encouraging comments you can share with a young person is to tell them you see potential in them.

When I was in middle school, a teacher remarked to me the potential she saw in me and encouraged me to work harder, to push myself more, and to read beyond my comfort zone. It's been decades since that happened, but I've never forgotten that conversation.

Potential is a powerful word to hear when you are young. But what about when you're older?

Can you imagine someone saying, "I saw potential in you back then—what happened?"

Unrealized potential is the field where regrets grow.

This quote by John Maxwell is one that has been a driver in my life for many years now: "Realizing your potential as a leader is *your* responsibility."[2] No one else's.

Weak people cast blame. They want to play the victim. It's always someone else's fault.

"They got the breaks—I didn't."

"They were lucky—I wasn't."

"They knew the right people—I didn't."

Catalytic leaders know the truth.

Winston Churchill said, "Continuous effort—not strength or intelligence—is the key to unlocking our potential."

It's up to you, leader.

Will you attain your potential?

I believe you are designed by God on purpose and for a purpose. To know your design and your purpose and to achieve it is the greatest source of satisfaction I know.

There is a famous quote that has been attributed to Mark Twain, though most now doubt that he was the source. "There are two great days in a person's life—the day we are born and the day we discover why." Regardless of who originated it, there is much truth there.

How are you designed? What is your purpose?

And what are you doing to unlock your potential?

The Last 10%

In his book, *The Leader's Greatest Return,* John Maxwell writes:

I read that when Jack Welch was the CEO of General Electric, he used to send out a memo to the incoming participants of the executive development course before they attended the first session. In it, he directed them to think about their answers to a group of questions that he wanted them to be ready to discuss. Here's what he wrote:

Tomorrow you are appointed CEO of GE:

What would you do in the first thirty days?

Do you have a current "vision" of what to do?

How would you go about developing one?

Present your best shot at the vision.

How would you go about "selling" the vision?

What foundations would you build on?

What current practices would you jettison?[3]

Can you imagine those conversations? I'd love to have been a fly on the wall for some of those.

Something I look for in our meetings and interactions is how honest team members will be with the feedback they share. Are they too polite to be honest? Are they too afraid to be honest? Do they consistently have helpful feedback? Is it delivered kindly and authentically?

Too often, "terminal niceness" is a plague that infects teams and organizations, especially in Christian-based organizational settings. We think "nice" is one of the fruits of the Spirit. It isn't.

As I've mentioned previously, my goal is for every member of our team to be able to share what we call "the last 10 percent." The first 90 percent of feedback is typically easy; it's that last 10 percent that we often hesitate to share. But I've learned that last 10 percent is where the truly transformational change is.

As you are on the lookout for emerging leaders in your organization, what traits are you looking for? What questions are you asking?

I believe the right questions lead us to the right answers. The wrong questions are too often the first ones we ask. Learning to ask good questions is a skill. It takes time, it takes energy, and it takes intentionality.

Again, from Maxwell's book: "Usually the people who can think, problem-solve, and communicate under pressure have good leadership potential—not all, but most. Sometimes you run across a good thinker and talker who's not a doer. And occasionally you find a good thinker and doer who has a tough time communicating. Nevertheless, ask questions. When you gather people, if all you do is give orders, all you will get is order takers. That's not what you want. You want leaders."[4]

Teaching Leaders

A few years ago, I had the privilege of sitting in a breakout session at the Re:Think Leadership Conference with one of my heroes in ministry, Dan Reiland. He is the Executive Pastor at 12Stone Church in Lawrenceville, Georgia. Dan previously partnered with John Maxwell for twenty years, first as

Executive Pastor at Skyline Wesleyan Church in San Diego, then as Vice President of Leadership and Church Development at INJOY. His talk that day focused on developing a leadership culture in your organization.

One of Dan's five essential elements to a leadership culture is that you **teach leadership**. The keys to this are simplicity and consistency.

If it's not **simple**, you will quit.

If it's not **consistent**, you won't get the results you want, and you will quit.

Leadership development is a "non-demand" ministry. It's not on fire or urgent. In other words, you could not do it. You can allow the have-to's to crowd out the don't-have-to's; you can allow the urgent to crowd out the important. But if you want a leadership culture in your organization, you must realize that though it's not on fire, it is in fact a must do.

Dan had some sage advice for us—get a group of people together (emerging leaders, existing leaders, staff, people in whom you see potential), pick a good leadership book to read together, and then when you meet (once a month), ask two questions:

1. What are you learning?

2. How do you apply what you're learning?[5]

So simple! You can do this. It takes intentionality—it's not going to happen without intentionality.

Don't allow yourself to overcomplicate the process— remember simplicity. Leadership development doesn't have to be overly complicated. In fact, less sticks when it is.

For example, I've regularly led a short-term IMPACT group for potential and emerging leaders at Southview. We read books together, we watch videos on leadership, and then we discuss. IMPACT has met weekly for sessions of six to ten weeks at least once a year, but I'm intrigued by Dan's suggestion of once a month. It's too easy to miss a meeting when it's weekly—once a month can be easier to commit to and prioritize. I might try that with our next group.

However you do it, in the famous words of Nike, Just Do It. And remember the key words—simplicity and consistency.

I'd highly recommend Dan's book, *Amplified Leadership*. It's a powerful book that you can take a group through.

Three Reminders for Developing Leaders

One of the things I love most about what I do is the opportunity to pour into new and developing leaders. I've only been leading for about three decades, but opportunities continue to arise for me to share with and advise young and emerging leaders. As I do, a common thread runs through many of these conversations, and I find myself returning again and again to three reminders that I share with them.

1. You're in a season of preparation. Listen more than you talk.

It is so tempting for new and emerging leaders to speak up—often! I remember so many times very early on in my leadership when I couldn't wait to speak up, to share what I knew was the greatest and freshest wisdom ever to be shared in a meeting from the beginning of time.

Probably not.

I think one of the greatest lessons I ever learned was the importance of listening. That's how you learn. And no one is born knowing how to lead—we all learn from somebody, somewhere. As you are in the early stages of growing and developing as a leader, listen. You may not (and probably won't) always agree with what you hear, but by listening, you can learn to discern what's helpful and what's not, to eat the fish and leave the bones.

2. Remember that a season of preparation is just that—a season.

You won't be here forever. There will likely come a time when others come to you for advice, to hear what you have to say. Right now, you have an opportunity to develop experience, insight, and wisdom, but only if you have a teachable spirit. That's a nonnegotiable for leaders where I lead—I can teach you a lot of things, but I cannot teach you to have a teachable spirit. You either have one or you don't. Make a conscious decision to have a teachable spirit, to avail yourself of this season of preparation to lead in the years and decades to come. Get around leaders who are better than you, who are further down the road than you are, and learn from them. Take advantage of the preparation season; you'll be so glad you did later when your season of leading arrives.

3. Read. Seriously.

You're not going to live long enough to make all the leadership mistakes yourself. Nor should you aspire to that. By reading about the lives and experiences of other leaders, you can learn to avoid many of the potholes they found themselves hitting. You can learn how to "go farther, faster," as Andy Stanley says, by learning from people who are farther down the leadership path than you are. John Maxwell said that "leaders are learners and leaders are readers,"[6] and he's spot on. If you can find a group of people who will read and discuss leadership books together, so much the better! Or maybe you can start one.

If you don't like to read, listen to audiobooks and podcasts. Don't let what you can't or don't like to do stop you from doing what you can. Focus on what you want *most* over what you want *now*. Remember, "No discipline seems pleasant at the time, but painful. Later on, however, it produces a harvest of righteousness and peace for those who have been trained by it" (Hebrews 12:11).

Chrysalis

Over the years, I've tried a lot of different ideas. Some worked; many did not. But if you don't throw the spaghetti at the wall, how will you know what will stick?

One of my favorite ideas was for an internship and residency program at Southview called Chrysalis.

College and seminary do a great job of preparing people for ministry academically, but in my experience, there is a significantly large gap between the academy and the ministry of the local church. I wanted to start a program where young leaders could come and "try it out." They would come on our staff team in a temporary role, be given responsibility and authority to lead in a specific area or project, be invested in by the leaders of our church, and see whether or not God was actively leading them into local church ministry.

Through that ministry idea, I saw young men and women come on our team, some hesitant, some confident. They would begin to take steps in their area of ministry, and as we would have the privilege of pouring into them, we would see them begin to grow and develop in their leadership gifts and skills. Just like every other spiritual gift, leadership is a gift that is given by the Holy Spirit. But it does not arrive fully developed, fully mature. It has to be exercised, tended, stretched, and grown over time. Through Chrysalis, I saw leaders develop and grow, moving on to other ministry assignments all across the country after they left us, impacting thousands of people through what God did in their lives.

Developing other leaders is not a nice add-on; it's what leaders do. It's part of the job description. It's part of the joy.

Give It Away

Benjamin Zander is the conductor for the Boston Philharmonic orchestra. I had the privilege of hearing Zander at a leadership conference in 2000 where he shared a simple but profound truth that I've never forgotten.

The conductor of an orchestra doesn't make a sound.

The goal of a conductor is to equip musicians to make the music—the conductor doesn't make any music. He invests in and works through the musicians to create the beautiful pieces that we are accustomed to hearing from an orchestra.

That's a *lot* like what a leader does.

Leaders don't—*can't* in fact—do everything. To quote the apostle Paul in his letter to the Ephesians Christians, the job of a pastor-leader is to equip people for works of service (Ephesians 4:12). But that principle will apply no matter the context. A leader invests in other leaders, recruiting, developing, encouraging, investing in, and equipping them to make their contribution to the organization's mission and purpose.

In an orchestra, the conductor directs the musicians to bring their best in each area, with the purpose and goal being that the combination of all those parts will create a powerful end result. So too does a leader invest in and direct other leaders to bring their best in what they lead, with the purpose and goal being that the combination of all those leadership efforts will create a powerful end result.

I like how Jim Collins talks about this. He writes, "We succeed and are our very best only when we help others succeed. That's how we build meaning. It's impossible to have a meaningful life without meaningful work."[7]

Andy Stanley has said, "The value of a life is always measured by how much of it was given away. . . . If your leadership isn't all about you, it will live beyond you. If it is all about you, it will not, other than that you will serve as someone's bad example."[8]

A catalytic leader develops other leaders, giving away what he or she has learned and investing it into other leaders to help them grow and thrive.

Chapter Twelve

Lead Yourself Well

T his final element of catalytic leadership might be the hardest of all: **leading yourself well.**

My experience is that I am the most difficult person to lead that I will ever lead. I bet you are the same. You are the most difficult person to lead that you will ever lead. And if you fail, it impacts so many others beyond just you. So, we have to get this right.

What does it look like to lead yourself catalytically?

1. Rest

I'm starting with this one because I know this is something most leaders struggle to do well.

Mark Buchanan wrote about how critical this is. He said, "Tiredness is a body thing. There's a goodness, a satisfaction to it. Weariness is a condition of the soul. I am weary of something. I stop caring about the things I care about."[1]

Weariness destroys a lot of leaders. Leading through the COVID pandemic took quite a few leaders off the field and onto the sidelines, from CEOs to pastors. Why? Because it was hard?

No. Because leaders worked harder than they might have ever before, and they saw fewer results from all that work. That's not only demotivating and discouraging, it's exhausting. And there was less patience on the part of the people they served. That's disheartening.

Many leaders tend to have problems rise to the top of their consciousness late at night, when there's nothing they can do about them. Bear in mind one of Colin Powell's leadership principles: "Things always look better in the morning. Get rest. Always be optimistic about what the next day will bring."[2]

Rest is the solution to a lot of self-leadership problems.

What's the reason so many leaders don't prioritize rest?

• Some think they have to put in more hours to get more done.
• Some think that if they rest, they're not maximizing their time.
• Some are so stressed that rest is elusive. They close their eyes but wake up repeatedly.

The challenge for leaders can be to stop, to let the day end.

I like what Jon Acuff said about this: "I don't get smarter the later I stay up."[3] I'm the same way. I do get grumpier, but not at all smarter. I have to let the day end, sleep, and then get up ready to rock and roll the next day.

For a long time, I struggled with this. I would get home, and I would bring with me all of my frustration at not getting everything done, at my lack of time, and sometimes at other people. I had to learn how to let go of those things on my way home so that I didn't bring them home with me. That was a challenge, and it didn't happen overnight. But it is possible.

I began to visualize hanging all the work stress up like a sack outside, not bringing it inside the house. It would still be there the next morning to pick up on my way out of the house to work, but I determined not to let it inside.

I was not perfect at this. Sometimes I would bring things in despite my desire not to. Sometimes I would find myself deep in thought about something at work and not "present" with my family. In those moments, I learned to give myself grace—make the decision again—and start fresh. You can do the same.

Rest matters. A good leader is a rested leader. I never make good decisions when I'm tired, and you won't either.

2. Reflect

If you are a person of faith like I am, then practicing daily spiritual disciplines is critical to leading yourself well. Reflecting on the previous day, week, or season can provide significant benefits. Remember, experience doesn't make you better. Evaluated experience makes you better. And that means reflection. We talked about this in Chapter Three, actively pursuing intentional growth.

Ask questions as you reflect, for example:

- What would a great leader have done in this situation?
- What can I learn from this for the next time I face something similar?

• What could it have meant if I had chosen something different in this situation? Think counterfactually—play out the scenario of alternate responses and decisions.

• If I didn't lead in this with excellence, what book can I read or what leader can I talk to about how to get better for the next time?

• Reflect on your life, leadership, character, faith, and who you are becoming. Am I getting better or just busier?

• What are the implications of my decision here for the legacy I want to leave, for the story I want to tell one day about this?

• What's the biggest learning from the week I just had?

• If I were going to teach a group of young leaders using this month's experiences, what lessons would I share?

Reflection can help you see things that you would have otherwise missed. You'll catch good actions and thoughts that you want to repeat; you'll catch actions and thoughts that need to be learned from and jettisoned, never to return. By reflecting on each day, you will learn and grow in wisdom, not just in age. Wisdom doesn't come automatically with age; it comes with reflection and evaluation.

3. Stay Physically Healthy

I'm primarily talking about diet and exercise here. Two areas that, when things get stressful, often fall to the wayside for many leaders.

Keeping this life gauge in the green zone can result in a 20 percent increase in stamina and achievement over time.

This also means leaders learn to manage their energy, not just their time.

John Maxwell notes, "People have uphill hopes and downhill habits."[4] Our results will come from our behaviors and habits. If we consistently make poor food choices and choose not to exercise, our health will reflect those choices.

Keep in mind the word I'm using: choices.

There is a very strong tendency to see ourselves as a victim, rather than the one who makes intentional choices, when it comes to our physical health. I want to gently but firmly push back on that.

I choose what I eat. I choose how much I exercise.

Are there times when it's more difficult than others? You bet!

Are there times when I am limited in my options? Absolutely.

Are there times when I just don't feel like it? Of course.

But with proper and prior planning, you and I can make better decisions in this area. The benefits are worth it.

4. Have Some Fun

Having an inspiring recreational activity outside my work world was not something on my radar or goal list ten years ago.

I was asked about this by my counselor once; she asked me what I did for fun. I completely blanked. "Read?" I said. She responded, "About work related stuff?" My response, "Well, yeah." She challenged me to find something recreational outside my work world, completely unrelated. So, I did. I took classes and learned how to shoot. Going to the gun range has become one of the most relaxing and enjoyable things that I've started doing in recent years. One of the things I love about it is that I can see the results of my work immediately. I can adjust when something's not working and see the results of that adjustment, good or bad, right then. I love that.

For a number of years, I tried running. I ran quite a few 5K races and had begun to train for a half marathon, but then I developed some micro tears in my Achilles tendon and decided that this was perhaps not the best recreational activity for me. Sometimes you try something, and it doesn't work. But you don't give up—you learn from it and move on to try something else.

Do you have something you do, just for you, recreationally? What relaxes you and brings you joy? You need to find what that is if you don't already know and do it. It's truly part of leading yourself well into a place of good health.

5. See a Counselor

Speaking of seeing a counselor . . .

I heard a senior leader say once many years ago: "If you are in leadership, and you are not seeing a counselor, you need to change that today."

I thought he was wrong. Why would I need to see a counselor?

Guess what? He knew what he was talking about.

I started seeing a counselor about seven years ago, and it's been so, so helpful. A counselor helps you navigate the present by dealing with the past, with what you've been through, and helps you process that which affects your present. Leaders, people are constantly backing up their dump trucks of problems to our office door and unloading. They drive away feeling much better, and what do we have? A floor full of other people's problems.

That has a cumulative effect. And if we're not processing all that and taking care of our own stuff too, well, that's a recipe for a ticking time bomb that *will* explode sooner or later. Above, we talked about physical health; this one has to do with maintaining emotional health. That's a gauge on the dashboard that some leaders ignore, but much like that pesky check engine light, ignoring it won't make the problem go away. As my friend Steve Kane says, "Bad news isn't like a fine wine; it doesn't get better with age."

Having someone to process the past and the present implications of it with has been helpful for me, and I strongly recommend regular counseling for leaders.

6. Get a Coach

Whom can you be 100 percent transparent with? Who will help you see what you cannot see?

Leaders, we are often in this role for others. We talk to and help others when they struggle or need coaching. But who helps us? Nearly 70 percent of leaders in a recent survey said no one, and they perceive that this loneliness and isolation affects their performance.[5]

It's hard to read the label when you're inside the bottle. It's hard to see the whole picture when you're in the frame.

I believe every leader needs someone to help them see what they can't see, to help them grow in their own self-awareness, and to help them think through and discover how to overcome the barriers and challenges that they face. We talked earlier in this book about the value of encouragement, where we pour courage into someone else. Who is doing that for you? It's difficult to lead others to a place of health and vitality where you've never been, or have only visited occasionally.

A counselor looks backward to help you process the past and thrive in the present. A coach helps you with the present looking forward into the future. That's what I do as I serve as a leadership coach for other leaders. I've had a leadership coach for many years now, so I know the power of this. That's one of the reasons why I've chosen to invest in leaders this way; I know the potential of coaching to help leaders intentionally grow and thrive. That helps everyone they lead.

What Are Your Guardrails?

Warren Buffet said, "It takes twenty years to build a reputation and five minutes to ruin it." And I think we have all seen leaders who were respected in their field, who had accomplished a great deal, and who were sidelined by a poor choice that they made in a moment.

Guardrails on the road serve to guide us and protect us from running into the ditch as we drive. They provide a barrier to keep us from something that could cause significant damage or even death. They're not necessarily pretty or attractive to look at, but they serve an incredibly important purpose.

Leaders, let me ask you: What are your guardrails?

Leading yourself well involves the creation and maintenance of guardrails in our lives. These could be moral guardrails, intended to prevent us from the ditch of marital infidelity. They could be financial guardrails, intended to protect us from the ditch of financial impropriety. They could be legal guardrails, intended to protect us from the ditch of shady decisions or even those that appear so.

Every leader needs guardrails to help protect them from the inadvertent, or sometimes purposefully chosen, ditches.

A lot of press was given to Vice President Mike Pence's public statement concerning the "Billy Graham rule," that he would not go out to eat alone with or meet alone with a member of the opposite sex (other than his wife). Whether you agree with the Vice President or not, this is a good example of a guardrail; something put in place to prevent you from driving into a ditch, accidentally or purposefully.

I have sought to build systems in place at Southview that will provide guardrails both for me as a leader and for our organization. For instance, I am not an authorized check signer. I can put in a check request, but I cannot sign it—someone else has to do that. The person who writes checks on our team is not authorized to sign them. And a third person, our CPA who can neither write nor sign checks, does the reconciliation for the bank statements each month. This system protects every person in the process by ensuring that no one person can authorize, write, sign a check, and then "disappear it" through a shady reconciliation process.

Who knows where you are all the time? Every person, and every leader especially, needs guardrails to keep them out of the ditches. Guardrails protect a leader from other people wrongfully accusing you or coming onto you in a one-on-one setting. Now, don't get me wrong: if a leader wants to blow past the guardrails, they can and will. No system is foolproof, particularly if a leader is determined to circumvent it. But it's so important to be mindful of the situations we step into.

I am weary of seeing leaders I have learned from and respected get sidelined by the choices that they make. I know that the implementation and execution of guardrails could have helped in many of those cases. But too often, leadership comes with a massive ego, reflected in thoughts like, "I'm good; I know those can be helpful for others, but I'm really beyond needing that."

I don't think *anyone* is beyond needing guardrails. That's part of leading yourself well.

The Power of a Picture

I like puzzles. Whether we're talking about sudoku, crosswords, or jigsaw puzzles, I'm a fan.

When I do jigsaw puzzles, I like to lay every piece out, face up, around the work area where I'm building the puzzle. My family thinks I'm a little strange to do that; it takes a while, but I think it's helpful!

Do you know what the most important part of the puzzle building process is for me? It's the picture on the box.

I set it prominently so I can see it while I work, and I utilize it frequently as I begin to assemble the picture that I see.

Leaders, this is what those on our teams often do with us. We are the picture. And they are assembling their leadership and habits based on the picture they see in us.

Leading ourselves well affects us primarily. That's really important. But it doesn't only affect us. It also affects all those we lead. Leading ourselves well then is part of leading our teams and organizations well.

Conclusion

I ntentional leadership is catalytic, and helping leaders to intentionally grow and thrive is my passion.

I want to see leaders cultivate a teachable spirit and make a significant impact and difference in their teams and their organizations.

I want to see leaders evaluate ruthlessly and aspire to proper productivity as they get better at leading; I agree with Craig Groeschel: "When a leader gets better, everybody benefits."[1]

I want to see leaders grow more intentionally, because growth doesn't just happen.

I want to see leaders discover who they are designed to be, how they were purposefully wired, so that they can lean into that design and wiring, not trying to be like anyone else, but being the best version of themselves that they can be.

I want to see leaders focus their bias for action, seeing it as a strength, not a weakness, that can and should be used to get things done.

I want to see leaders choose to be family-focused, making their priorities clear to those who matter most.

I want to see leaders build up the people and teams they lead, understanding that encouragement is critical to success.

I want to see leaders step up on leading change, developing other leaders, and prioritizing clear communication with those they lead.

Are you ready to do what it takes to become a catalytic leader?

I hope this book has informed and begun to equip you in your journey toward that goal. I would be honored to serve you and your team through my Catalytic Leadership Coaching and speaking, should you be ready for that next step. You can find out more at catalyticleadership.net.

Additional Resources

When I first started to study leadership and first began to lead, I had to struggle to find a lot of great leadership material. That's no longer the case! Below are some of the podcasts, books, and conferences I recommend regularly to leaders.

Podcasts

- *The Andy Stanley Leadership Podcast*
- *The Craig Groeschel Leadership Podcast*
- *The John Maxwell Leadership Podcast*
- *The Carey Nieuwhof Leadership Podcast*
- *The Courage to Lead Podcast* with Shawn Lovejoy
- *The Working Genius Podcast* with Patrick Lencioni
- *The Unstuck Church Podcast* with Tony Morgan
- *All It Takes Is a Goal* with Jon Acuff
- *WorkLife* with Adam Grant
- *Revisionist History* with Malcolm Gladwell

Books

• *The 21 Irrefutable Laws of Leadership* by John C. Maxwell

• *Developing the Leader Within You 2.0* by John C. Maxwell

• *Death by Meeting* by Patrick Lencioni

• *The Ideal Team Player* by Patrick Lencioni

• *Visioneering* by Andy Stanley

• *Choosing to Cheat* by Andy Stanley

• *Communicating for a Change* by Andy Stanley and Lane Jones

• *Leading Change Without Losing It* by Carey Nieuwhof

• *Didn't See It Coming* by Carey Nieuwhof

• *Getting Things Done* by David Allen

• *Humilitas* by John Dickson

• *Soundtracks* by Jon Acuff

• *Know What You're FOR* by Jeff Henderson

• *Good to Great* by Jim Collins

• Get your free copy of *The Performance Practice* at https://www.leapambassadors.org/continuous-improvement/performance-practice.

• *I Said This, You Heard That* by Kathleen Edelman, resources at isaidyouheard.study

Conferences/Workshops

• The Global Leadership Summit
• Leadercast

- Drive (for church leaders)
- Live2Lead
- The Disney Institute: Disney's Approach to Leadership Excellence

Acknowledgments

I must begin by acknowledging the incredible love and support from my wife, Charlotte, and our daughters, Erin and Allison. They were beyond kind and patient with me during the writing and editing as I wrapped this project up. They have provided more encouragement than I could ask for.

I am so grateful for the leaders I've had the privilege of learning from for the last thirty plus years. To name them all would take a book this size and then some.

Thank you to my editor, Carly Catt, who has been a joy to work with on this project. She made the writing better and so much clearer; every reader will be grateful for her efforts. I surely am.

Thank you to the staff of Southview Community Church, whom I have the joy of leading. They teach me more about leadership every day, and it's wonderful to serve others alongside such a committed and mission-driven team.

And thank you to the people who call Southview home, who have encouraged me in my own leadership journey. I love following Jesus with you.

About the Author

William Attaway has been married to his amazing wife Charlotte for twenty-four years, with whom he has two beautiful daughters who are truly gifts from God. He's a Leadership Coach for Catalytic Leadership, LLC, a company he founded to help leaders to grow *intentionally* and thrive. He currently serves as the lead pastor at Southview Community Church in Herndon, Virginia (just outside Washington, D.C.), where he has served for the last seventeen years. He's a John Maxwell Team certified speaker, coach, and trainer, and has taught courses in Old and New Testament Survey and the Pentateuch for Washington University of Virginia and Itawamba Community College. He holds a Ph.D. in Old Testament (with an emphasis in Biblical Backgrounds and Archaeology) and has worked for two seasons on the team of an archaeological dig at Tall el-Hammam in Jordan. He's also the author of *Lead: Leadership Lessons from the (Not So) Minor Prophets* (Eriall Press, 2014).

Endnotes by Chapter

Introduction

1. Brian Herbert, *House Harkonnen* (New York, NY: Spectra Books, 2001).

2. Jim Collins, *Great by Choice: Uncertainty, Chaos, and Luck —Why Some Thrive Despite Them All* (New York, NY: Harper Business, 2011).

Chapter One: Cultivate a Teachable Spirit

1. Andy Stanley, "Uniquely Better" (Global Leadership Summit, South Barrington, IL, August 2017).

2. Warren Bennis, *On Becoming a Leader* (New York, NY: Basic Books, 2009).

3. Marcus Buckingham, *The One Thing You Need to Know* (New York, NY: Simon and Schuster, 2008).

4. Colin Powell, *It Worked For Me: In Life and Leadership* (New York, NY: Harper Perennial, 2014).

5. Craig Groeschel, "How the Best Leaders Think" (webinar teaching, October 2021).

6. Larry King, *How to Talk to Anyone, Anytime, Anywhere: The Secrets of Good Communication* (New York, NY: Crown, 1995).

7. Stanley, "Uniquely Better."

8. Darren Hardy, *The Compound Effect* (New York, NY: Hachette Books, 2010).

9. John C. Maxwell, *Good Leaders Ask Great Questions* (New York, NY: Center Street, 2014).

10. John. C. Maxwell, *Developing the Leader Within You 2.0* (Nashville, TN: HarperCollins Leadership, 2018).

11. Warren Bennis, "Leading in an Age of Vulnerability (Global Leadership Summit, South Barrington, IL, August 2002).

12. John Dickson, *Humilitas: A Lost Key to Life, Love, and Leadership* (Grand Rapids, Michigan: Zondervan, 2011).

13. John Ortberg, "The Seduction of the Leader" (Global Leadership Summit, South Barrington, IL, August 2002).

14. Ortberg, "The Seduction of the Leader."

15. Jon Acuff, *Do Over: Rescue Monday, Reinvent Your Work, and Never Get Stuck* (New York, NY: Portfolio/Penguin, 2015).

16. Craig Groeschel, *Craig Groeschel Leadership Podcast.*

17. Patrick Lencioni, *The Five Dysfunctions of a Team* (San Francisco, CA: Jossey-Bass, 2002).

Chapter Two: Discover Your Wiring

1. Patrick Lencioni, "The Most Dangerous Mistakes Leaders Make" (Global Leadership Summit, South Barrington, IL, August 2014).

2. Benjamin E. Mays, *Quotable Quotes of Benjamin E. Mays* (Burlington, VT: Vantage Press, 1983).

3. "Benjamin Mays," Wikipedia, accessed November 22, 2021, https://en.wikipedia.org/wiki/Benjamin_Mays.

4. "Benjamin Mays."

5. The John C. Maxwell Company, "Man in the Mirror," *John C. Maxwell Blog*, published October 1, 2014, https://www.johnmaxwell.com/blog/man-in-the-mirror.

6. "An Introduction to the Input® CliftonStrengths Theme," (website), accessed November 12, 2021, https://www.gallup.com/cliftonstrengths/en/252278/input-theme.aspx/.

7. "An Introduction to the Learner® CliftonStrengths Theme," (website), accessed November 12, 2021, https://www.gallup.com/cliftonstrengths/en/252293/learner-theme.aspx/.

Chapter Three: Actively Pursue Intentional Growth

1. Carey Nieuwhof, (Re:Think Leadership Conference, Atlanta, Georgia, May 2017).

2. Mark Miller, *Win Every Day: Proven Practices for Extraordinary Results* (Oakland, CA: Berrett-Koehler Publishers, Inc., 2020).

3. "Invest in Your Strengths," *Marcus Buckingham Blog*, April 11, 2018, https://www.marcusbuckingham.com/invest-in-your-strengths-2.

4. John Maxwell, *Sometimes You Win, Sometimes You Learn* (New York, NY: Center Street, 2013).

5. Seth Godin, (Global Leadership Summit, South Barrington, IL, August 2011).

6. Jeff Immelt, *Hot Seat: What I Learned Leading a Great American Company* (New York, NY: Avid Reader Press, 2021).

7. Jim Collins, *Good to Great: Why Some Companies Make the Leap… and Others Don't* (New York, NY: Harper Business, 2001).

8. Ed Catmull, *Creativity, Inc.: Overcoming the Unseen Forces That Stand in the Way of True Inspiration* (New York, NY: Random House, 2014).

9. Aja Brown, (Leadercast Conference, Atlanta, GA, May 2015).

10. "About Us," *Leap of Reason* (website), accessed November 15, 2021, https://leapofreason.org/about-us-2/.

11. "Performance Practice," *Leap of Reason Ambassadors Community* (website), accessed December 19, 2021, https://www.leapambassadors.org/continuous-improvement/performance-practice/.

12. "Performance Practice."

13. John Maxwell, *The 21 Indispensable Qualities of a Leader* (Nashville, TN: Thomas Nelson Publishers, 1999).

14. University of Tokyo. "Study shows stronger brain activity after writing on paper than on tablet or smartphone: Unique, complex information in analog methods likely gives brain more details to trigger memory." *ScienceDaily*. www.sciencedaily.com/releases/2021/03/210319080820.htm (accessed December 18, 2021).

Chapter Four: Be Boldly Action-Oriented

1. Clay Scroggins, guest, "Clay Scroggins on How to Lead When You're Not in Charge," *Carey Nieuwhof Leadership Podcast*, Episode 153, August 14, 2017.

2. Len Schlesinger, Paul Brown, Charles Kiefer, *Own Your Future: How to Think Like an Entrepreneur and Thrive in an Unpredictable Economy* (New York, NY: Amacom Books, 2014).

3. Dr. Brené Brown, *Rising Strong: How the Ability to Reset Transforms the Way We Live, Love, Parent, and Lead* (New York, NY: Random House, 2017).

4. Tony Dungee, *Quiet Strength: The Principles, Practices & Priorities of a Winning Life* (Carol Stream, IL: Tyndale

Momentum, 2008).

5. Aja Brown, (Leadercast Conference, Atlanta, GA, May 2015).

6. Dr. Brené Brown, "Rising Strong" (Global Leadership Summit, South Barrington, IL, August 2015).

7. John Ortberg, "The Seduction of the Leader" (Global Leadership Summit, South Barrington, IL, August 2002).

Chapter Five: Choose to Be Family-Focused

1. David Allen, *Getting Things Done: The Art of Stress-Free Productivity* (London, England: Penguin Books, 2002).

2. Dr. Brené Brown, "Rising Strong" (Global Leadership Summit, South Barrington, IL, August 2015).

3. Andy Stanley, *Better Decisions, Fewer Regrets: 5 Questions to Help You Determine Your Next Move* (Grand Rapids, MI: Zondervan, 2020).

Chapter Six: Evaluate Ruthlessly

1. Miller, *Win Every Day*.

2. Andy Stanley, "Leading with Boldness" (Leadercast Conference, Atlanta, GA, May 2015).

3. Mark Batterson, *In a Pit with a Lion on a Snowy Day* (Colorado Springs, CO: Multnomah, 2008).

4. Stanley, "Leading with Boldness."

5. John Maxwell, (Leadercast Conference, Atlanta, GA, May 2012).

6. Jim Collins, "When Business Thinking Fails the Church" (The Leadership Summit, South Barrington, IL, August 2006).

7. Collins, "When Business Thinking Fails the Church."

8. David Gergen, "Eyewitness to Power" (The Leadership Summit, South Barrington, IL, August 2009).

9. Andy Stanley, "Beyond You Leadership" (Leadercast Conference, Atlanta, GA, May 2014).

Chapter Seven: Aspire for Proper Productivity

1. Craig Groeschel, (Catalyst One Day conference, October 2017).

2. "Pareto Principle," Investopedia, December 25, 2020, https://www.investopedia.com/terms/p/paretoprinciple.asp.

3. Barrie Markham Rhodes, "Canute (Knud) The Great," *The Viking Network*, published June 22, 2015, https://www.viking.no/the-viking-kings-and-earls/canute-knud-the-great.

4. Bob Buford, *Drucker & Me: What a Texas Entrepreneur Learned From the Father of Modern Management* (Brentwood, TN: Worthy Books, 2014).

5. Buford, *Drucker & Me.*

6. Buford, *Drucker & Me.*

Chapter Eight: Build Up People and Teams

1. Collins, *Good to Great.*

2. "What's Wrong with Social Distancing?" Tim Elmore, *Growing Leaders* (blog), April 22, 2020, https://growingleaders.com/blog/whats-wrong-with-social-distancing/.

3. Dan Reiland, "Encouragement is 51% of Leadership," *Dan Reiland* (website), accessed December 19, 2021, https://danreiland.com/encouragement-leadership/.

4. Andy Stanley, "Beyond You Leadership" (Leadercast Conference, Atlanta, GA, May 2014).

5. Stanley, "Beyond You Leadership."

6. Horst Shultze, (Global Leadership Summit, South Barrington, IL, August 2015).

7. Collins, *Good to Great.*

8. I first heard this taught in 2000 at the Global Leadership Summit as the 3 Cs, and I've added two of my own in the years since based on my own experience, frustrations, and learning.

9. Brandon Gaille, "19 Employee Motivation Statistics and Trends," *Brandon Gaille Small Business & Marketing Advice* (website), accessed December 19, 2021,

https://brandongaille.com/17-employee-motivation-statistics-and-trends/.

10. Craig Groeschel, (Global Leadership Summit, South Barrington, IL, August 2015).

11. Carey Nieuwhof, "Why the Smartest Leaders Move Way Beyond Their To-Do List to Tackle This," *Carey Nieuwhof* (website), September 2019, https://careynieuwhof.com/why-the-smartest-leaders-move-way-beyond-their-to-do-list-to-tackle-this/.

12. Carey Nieuwhof, "What Determines Your True Potential? (You Might Be Surprised)," *Carey Nieuwhof* (website), September 2014, https://careynieuwhof.com/what-determines-your-true-potential-you-might-be-surprised/.

13. Daniel Goleman, *Emotional Intelligence: Why It Can Matter More Than IQ* (New York, NY: Random House, 2005).

14. Buford, *Drucker & Me*.

15. "The Cost of a Bad Hire," *Northwestern* (website), February 2019, https://www.northwestern.edu/hr/about/news/february-2019/the-cost-of-a-bad-hire.html/.

16. "The Cost of a Bad Hire Can Be Astronomical," SHRM (website), May 9, 2017, https://www.shrm.org/resourcesandtools/hr-topics/employee-relations/pages/cost-of-bad-hires.aspx/.

17. "Now is the Time for Leaders to Step Up," *Growing Leaders Blog*, published October 12, 2021, https://growingleaders.com/blog/now-is-the-time-for-leaders-to-step-up/?mc_cid=8ced55f3df&mc_eid=eb3f880453.

18. Dave Ramsey, guest, "Q&A with Dave Ramsey: Winning, Failing, and Success," *Craig Groeschel Leadership Podcast*, Episode 86, February 4, 2021.

19. Stephen Covey, *The 7 Habits of Highly Effective People* (New York, NY: Free Press, 1989).

20. John C. Maxwell, *Good Leaders Ask Great Questions* (New York, NY: Center Street, 2014). Emphasis added.

21. Shultze, (Global Leadership Summit).

Chapter Nine: Never Stop Leading Change

1. Carey Nieuwhof, (Orange Conference, Atlanta, Georgia, April 2015).

2. Jack Welch, (Global Leadership Summit, South Barrington, IL, August 2010).

3. John Maxwell, (Leadercast Conference, Atlanta, GA, May 2012).

4. Collins, *Good to Great*.

5. Max DePree, *Leadership Is An Art* (Redfern, New South Wales: Currency, 2004).

6. Buford, *Drucker & Me*.

7. Craig Groeschel, "It" (Global Leadership Summit, South Barrington, IL, August 2008).

8. John Maxwell, (Live2Lead Conference, Atlanta, GA, October 2018).

9. Andy Stanley, *Visioneering* (Sisters, Oregon: Multnomah, 1999).

10. Martin Luther King Jr., "The Death of Evil upon the Seashore," (sermon given at the Cathedral of St. John the Divine, New York City, May 17, 1956).

11. Rorke Denver, (Leadercast Conference, Atlanta, Georgia, May 2015).

12. Andy Stanley, (Leadercast Conference, Atlanta, Georgia, May 2012).

13. Jeff Henderson, (Re:Think Leadership Conference, Atlanta, Georgia, May 2017).

14. Jonathan Milligan, *Your Message Matters: How to Rise Above the Noise and Get Paid For What You Know* (Ada, Michigan: Baker Books, 2020).

15. Carey Nieuwhof, (Re:Think Leadership Conference, Atlanta, Georgia, May 2017).

16. Malala Yousafzai, (Leadercast Conference, Atlanta, Georgia, May 2015).

17. Denver, (Leadercast Conference).

18. Dina Gerdman, "COVID Killed the Traditional Workplace. What Should Companies Do Now?" *Harvard Business School*, March 8, 2021, https://hbswk.hbs.edu/item/covid-killed-the-traditional-workplace-what-should-companies-do-now?

cid=spmailing-33132823-WK%20Newsletter%20-%20One-
Off%20Mailing%203-8-21%20(1)-March%2008,%202021.

Chapter Ten: Prioritize Clear Communication

1. Ken Davis, (Communicating in Today's Reality Conference,
South Barrington, IL, October 2003).

2. Davis, (Communicating in Today's Reality Conference).

3. Davis, (Communicating in Today's Reality Conference).

4. Davis, (Communicating in Today's Reality Conference).

5. Dave Ramsey, guest, "Q&A with Dave Ramsey: Winning,
Failing, and Success," *Craig Groeschel Leadership Podcast*,
Episode 86, February 4, 2021.

6. Marcus Buckingham, *One Thing You Need to Know: About
Great Managing, Great Leading, and Sustained Individual
Success* (New York, NY: Free Press, 2005).

Chapter Eleven: Develop Other Leaders

1. Craig Groeschel, (Catalyst One Day Conference, October
2016).

2. John Maxwell, (Global Leadership Summit, South
Barrington, IL, August 2018). Emphasis added.

3. John C. Maxwell, *The Leader's Greatest Return: Attracting,
Developing, and Multiplying Leaders* (Nashville, TN:

HarperCollins Leadership, 2020).

4. Maxwell, *The Leader's Greatest Return*.

5. Dan Reiland, (Re:Think Leadership Conference, Atlanta, Georgia, May 2017).

6. Maxwell, (Global Leadership Summit).

7. Jim Collins, "Seven Questions: Beyond Good to Great" (Global Leadership Summit, South Barrington, IL, August 2015)

8. Andy Stanley, (Leadercast Conference, Atlanta, Georgia, May 2014).

Chapter Twelve: Lead Yourself Well

1. Mark Buchanan, "Sustainability: The Rest of God" (Ancient-Future Community GroupLife Conference, South Barrington, IL, September 2007).

2. Colin Powell, (Global Leadership Summit, South Barrington, IL, August 2013).

3. Jon Acuff, (Re:Think Leadership Conference, Atlanta, Georgia, May 2017).

4. John Maxwell, (Global Leadership Summit, South Barrington, IL, August 2018).

5. "Why Lonely Leaders Are Bad for Business—How Coaches Can Help," *Ray Williams* (website), accessed December 19,

2021, https://raywilliams.ca/why-lonely-leaders-are-bad-for-business-how-coaches-can-help/.

Conclusion

1. Craig Groeschel, (Global Leadership Summit, South Barrington, IL, August 2021).

Connect with William

CatalyticLeadership.net

LinkedIn.com/in/WilliamAttaway

Facebook.com/CatalyticLeadershipLLC

Twitter.com/WilliamAttaway

Ready For Your Next Step?

Would you like to work with William?

Set up a call today to begin your leadership coaching journey with William,

and experience the power of coaching to help you

grow *intentionally* and thrive like never before.

CATALYTICLEADERSHIP.NET/DISCOVERYCALL

Made in the USA
Las Vegas, NV
09 March 2022

45252836R10125